MARK CHAMPKINS
Foreword by PETER JONES

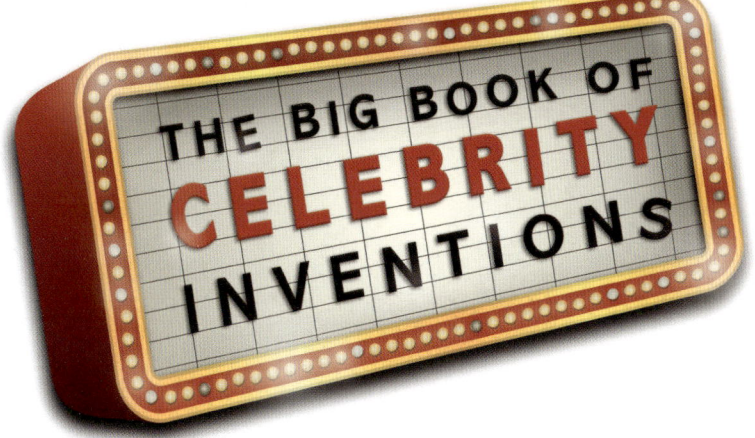

HarperCollins*Publishers*

HarperCollins*Publishers*
77–85 Fulham Palace Road,
Hammersmith, London, W6 8JB

www.harpercollins.co.uk

First published by HarperCollins*Publishers* 2011
1 3 5 7 9 10 8 6 4 2
© Mark Champkins 2011

Mark Champkins asserts the moral right to be identified as the author of this work

A catalogue record of this book is available in the British Library

ISBN 978-0-00-736276-9

Printed and bound in Great Britain by Butler Tanner & Dennis Ltd, Frome, Somerset

All rights reserved. No part of this publication may be reproduced, stored in a retrieval system, or transmitted, in any form or by any means, electronic, mechanical, photocopying, recording or otherwise, without the prior written permission of the publishers.

Cover photographs © Joe Alvarez (Nicola Roberts); Chris Terry (Jamie Oliver); Charles Sykes/Rex Features (Charlie Sheen); JoelAnderson.com (Peter Jones); Eugene Adebari/Rex Features (Michael Jackson); Liberation Foods (Harry Hill); Sipa Press/Rex Features (Prince)

Cover illustrations © Jerram Clifford; Shutterstock

Internal photography © the following: pp.14, 17, 26, 34, 38, 39, 42, 44, 48, 56, 64, 68, 71, 122, 130, 134, 142 © Rex Features; pp.18, 30, 60, 90, 104, 160 © NI Syndication; p.7 JoelAnderson.com; p.10 Fizz @ Lucid Picture; pp.11–12 Karl Pilkington; pp.22–24 Liberation Foods Ltd; p.52 Sandrine Dulermo and Michael Labica; p.74 Jon Snow; p.78 Johnny Ball; p.82 Kirsten O'Brien/Wise Buddah; p.86 Suzi Perry/Stewart Bywater; p.94 Lisa Rogers; p.100 Chris Terry; p.112 Charley Boorman; p.115 Charley Boorman; pp.126–129 Dyson; p.150 Paul Smith; pp.151–153 Chivas Brothers; pp.156–159 JoelAnderson.com; p.164 Innocent Smoothies; p.172 Martha Lane Fox; p.174 envirowarrior.com; p.176 Yo Company; pp.184–186 Tony Benn; p.188 Mark Champkins; p.192 Jerram Clifford
The following images © Wikicommons and: p.25 Jonwood2; p.49 Davidhv22; p.51 Producer; p.59 Morgon Tupp; p.62 Archos; pp.66–67 Bainzy; p.75 Mark Ramsey; pp.80–81 Jason Gaviria; p.87 Edward; p.108 Smithsonian Institution; p.131 Telrunya; p.138 Alan Fisher

Other images © the following: p.15 Krzysztof Isbrandt; p.18 Michal Zacharzewski; p.19 Megan Stevens; p.20 Kristin Smith; p.21 Jon Syverson; p.25 Hernan Herrero; p.31 Jori Valentina; p.33 Jos van Galen; p.36 Simon Gray, Eric Ortner, Jonathan Werner; p.40 Laura Glover; p.46 Dimitri Castrique Ploegsteert; p.47 Charlie Balch; pp.52–55 Jori Valentina; p.59 Paul Tonner; p.80 Antonio Jiménez Alonso; p.85 David Duncan; p.88 Jayanta Behera; p.97 Mark Anderson; p.100 Martin Walls; p.109 Julie Elliott-Abshire; p.110 Yaroslav B.; p.111 Ahmed Al-Shukaili; p.113 Orcun Tahtali; p.114 Victoria Herrera; p.123 Kriss Szkurlatowski; p.125 Nicolas Sales, Vladimir P.; p.132 Kriss Szkurlatowski; p.133 Andrzej Pobiedzinski; p.136 Martin Walls; p.137 Kim McLeod; p.140 Mohamed Ally; p.145 Kriss Szkurlatowki, Heather Sorenson; p.147 Joel Kingsbury; p.161 Giuseppe C.; p.178 Lorenzo Gonzalez; p.182 Simon Cataudo, Esra Su

Internal illustration © Jerram Clifford

While every effort has been made to trace the owners of copyright material reproduced herein and secure permissions, the publishers would like to apologise for any omissions and will be pleased to incorporate missing acknowledgements in any future editions of this book.

FSC™ is a non-profit international organisation established to promote the responsible management of the world's forests. Products carrying the FSC label are independently certified to assure consumers that they come from forests that are managed to meet the social, economic and ecological needs of present and future generations, and other controlled sources.

Find out more about HarperCollins and the environment at
www.harpercollins.co.uk/green

1. ACTORS & COMEDIANS

KARL PILKINGTON	10
CHARLIE SHEEN	14
STEVE MCQUEEN	18
HARRY HILL	22
MARLON BRANDO	26
RUBY WAX	30
JAMIE LEE CURTIS	34
PAUL NEWMAN	38

2. MUSICIANS & DIRECTORS

MICHAEL JACKSON	44
JAMES CAMERON	48
NICOLA ROBERTS	52
PRINCE	56
FRANCIS FORD COPPOLA	60
EDDIE VAN HALEN	64
GEORGE LUCAS	68

3. TV PERSONALITIES

JON SNOW	74
JOHNNY BALL	78
KIRSTEN O'BRIEN	82
SUZI PERRY	86
PETER SNOW	90
LISA ROGERS	94

4. COOKS & SHOWMEN

JAMIE OLIVER	100
HESTON BLUMENTHAL	104
HARRY HOUDINI	108
CHARLEY BOORMAN	112
URI GELLER	116

5. ARTISTS, DESIGNERS & WRITERS

ROALD DAHL	122
JAMES DYSON	126
ANDY WARHOL	130
ORLA KIELY	134
WALT DISNEY	138
DONATELLA VERSACE	142
MARK TWAIN	146
PAUL SMITH	150

6. BUSINESS PEOPLE & PUBLIC FIGURES

PETER JONES	156
MARGARET THATCHER	160
ADAM BALON	164
ABRAHAM LINCOLN	168
MARTHA LANE FOX	172
SIMON WOODROFFE	176
PRINCE CHARLES	180
TONY BENN	184

FOREWORD
BY PETER JONES

When I was approached by the BBC in 2004 about *Dragons' Den*, I decided to get involved because I've always had an interest in innovation and invention and I love gadgets, gismos and new technology.

Being a Dragon, as you might imagine, I have had all manner of strange inventions pitched at me from 'edible greeting cards for dogs' to 'rollerskates that you wear on your knees'.

I suspect most people have an idea for a new product or invention lurking in the back of their mind. However, in my experience, having the idea is not the hard part: developing and commercializing an invention makes up the majority of the work. Thomas Edison said 'genius is 1% inspiration and 99% perspiration'.

As an investor in inventive ideas, I like to ensure that I provide all the time, space and resources for my investee to work hard and succeed. If I decide to invest in an inventor's ideas, I need to feel like I can really contribute something.

When I saw Mark Champkins come into the Den, I thought he looked like an inventor if ever I saw one. All he needed was a little bow tie that span round. In his pitch he kept unveiling more and more products, saying, 'and here's another thing I've designed… and here's another…' I decided to invest because I knew that he would come up with ideas that would really take off, because I felt that I had the contacts and infrastructure to help him. Since then, he's expanded the business, is working with the Science Museum as their 'Inventor in Residence' and has written this book about invention. It's worked out well.

One major thing I have learnt through watching pitches in the Den is that you can learn a great deal about somebody from their inventions, and that's also true of the celebrities in this book. Their inventions provide intriguing insights about their character, and reveal a side they don't show on the red carpet. Who would have thought that Jamie Lee Curtis would invent a nappy, or that Marlon Brando would make a device for tuning bongo drums?

I find it fascinating that celebrities at the height of their career would, out of the public gaze, seek to address the problems in their lives through inventions. I think it says something about their desire to have an impact on the world, and it demonstrates the industriousness that is probably the driving factor behind their prominence.

In this book some of the most amazing inventions dreamt up by famous figures have been investigated. Mark explores their ideas, the stories behind their inspiration and how the inventions have been – or could be – developed. You may think you already know these celebrities, but their inventions throw a new light on their lives and interests.

This book is a celebration of oddness, originality and ingenuity. I hope that it will fascinate, baffle, amuse and, ultimately, inspire you.

1. ACTORS & COMEDIANS

KARL PILKINGTON

THE CLIPPABLE COASTER

STAR OF SKY 1'S *AN IDIOT ABROAD* AND AUTHOR OF BOOKS SUCH AS *KARLOLOGY* AND *HAPPYSLAPPED BY A JELLYFISH*, KARL ROSE TO FAME FOR HIS CONTRIBUTIONS TO THE HUGELY POPULAR PODCAST *THE RICKY GERVAIS SHOW* WITH RICKY GERVAIS AND STEPHEN MERCHANT. HAVING SOMETHING OF A GIFT FOR SEEING THE WORLD IN A DIFFERENT WAY, KARL'S UNIQUE STYLE OF THINKING HAS LED HIM TO INVENT THE CLIPPABLE COASTER.

> In our house we always have a problem. We don't have any saucers. This means that whenever I'm having a cup of tea, I have to use books and other items to avoid staining wooden tables. I'm fed up with that.
>
> I've had an idea for a clippable coaster. Basically it's a mat that clips the bottom of your cup. It's made in lots of sizes for different size of cups. No matter where you put your cup down, the surface will be protected from the heat – as the mat never leaves it. They are also dishwasher proof.

Karl was described by the *Telegraph* as 'AN IDIOT PHILOSOPHER'. His ideas and opinions have ranged so widely that there is actually a Wikipedia-style 'Pilkipedia', dedicated to recording his thoughts and latest activities.

The clippable coaster is one in a long line of his intriguing ideas, observations and questions, including 'PARROTS HAVE GONE A BIT QUIET SINCE PIRATES HAVE GONE', 'A SEAL IS SOMEWHERE BETWEEN A FISH AND A DOG' and 'WHAT ARE THOSE THINGS IN GREMLINS CALLED?' So is the Clippable Coaster useful or just plain daft?

THE DESIGN DETAILS

Karl's coaster design has four springy arms, which means it can grip differently sized cups and stay attached to the cup wherever it goes, to catch drips and stop them marking furniture.

So, why not just use a saucer? Karl's coaster has the advantage of staying attached to the cup, which makes it much easier to manage. It only ever requires one hand, leaving your other hand free, which, in fact, has a distinct safety advantage, if you think about it. Settling down for a cup of tea and a biscuit may be more dangerous than you imagine, and having a free hand may help prevent injury. In 2009,

Clippable mat.

a study revealed that 25 million people in Britain hurt themselves on tea breaks, with biscuits proving to be particularly dangerous elements responsible for many of these injuries.

While 25% of this number scalded themselves with hot drinks, 3% poked themselves in the eye whilst drinking, 7% were bitten by a pet trying to get their biscuit and one man ended up getting stuck in wet concrete after wading in to pick up a stray biscuit. In the face of these statistics, Karl's design could in fact make Britain a safer place.

COASTING THROUGH HISTORY

Karl's innovation comes from a long line of tweaks to a concept that was thought to have originated in the efficient and sophisticated civilization of the Romans. Fascinatingly, fragments of early stone coasters were found in the ruins of Pompeii.

More recently, there have been hundreds of coaster-based inventions. There are coasters that change colour when they come into contact with liquid, versions that glow in the dark and designs that actually keep liquid hot or cold. There have been patents for musical coasters, coasters made from old CDs and even coasters that smell like bar snacks – designed to make beer drinkers feel hungry.

Much to Ricky Gervais' and Stephen Merchant's amusement, Karl has stated that he'd like to commercially launch his contribution to coaster innovation, and he is keen to find the right manufacturing partner. So watch this space.

THE PERFECT CUPPA

Here are some other ideas that might revolutionize the tea break:

1. Tea bags that include the right proportions of sugar and milk powder to suit your taste – you will always get the perfect cuppa, wherever you are, no matter what isn't in the fridge.

2. Teapot-sized teabags – get multiple cuppas from one bag.

3. Teacup thermostat – a cup that keeps your brew at the perfect temperature.

4. Tea-leaf-infused biscuits – dunking these in your tea will make its flavour stronger.

5. Teacup cosies (with the option for it to enclose your hand too) – ideal for keeping your hands warm in winter and your drink hotter longer.

CHARLIE SHEEN

THE LIP-BALM DISPENSER

HOLLYWOOD ACTOR CHARLIE SHEEN HAS A COLOURFUL PAST. THOUGH HE'S STARRED IN A STRING OF SUCCESSFUL FILMS AND SITCOMS FROM *PLATOON* AND *HOT SHOTS* TO *TWO AND A HALF MEN*, AND WAS AT ONE POINT REPORTEDLY THE HIGHEST-PAID ACTOR IN HOLLYWOOD. IN RECENT YEARS HIS NAME HAS BECOME MORE SYNONYMOUS WITH ERRATIC BEHAVIOUR THAN WITH ACTING.

This is not a new development. Charlie's been in and out of rehab for drug and alcohol addiction since the late 1990s, but in an interview in early 2011 he demonstrated his increasingly odd perception about his life when he claimed he was 'on a drug called Charlie Sheen' and that he had 'tiger blood'.

HOWEVER, HIS BIZARRE ACTIONS AREN'T CONFINED TO HIS HOLLYWOOD EXPLOITS. Over the last two decades Charlie has copyrighted a series of strange phrases, has leveraged the Sheen family name to launch a number of improbable product lines and has patented an unlikely invention to assist the soothing of chapped lips.

LIP SERVICE

CHARLIE'S CREATIVE OUTPOURING STARTED IN THE LATE 1990S when he was living in the ski resort of Aspen, Colorado. As a keen skier and snowboarder, he identified a problem with having to re-apply lip balm throughout the day to prevent getting chapped lips. Frustrated with having to take his gloves on and off in the cold to manipulate the tube's winding mechanism, and in doing so regularly losing the caps, Charlie designed a solution.

In 1999 he filed a patent for a **'CHAPSTICK-DISPENSING APPARATUS'** with a 'slidably, pivotably, or hingeably attached' cap which cannot get lost. To replace the fiddly winding mechanism, he designed a chunky slider with which the lip-balm stick can be exposed or retracted – even whilst wearing gloves. Finally he added a lanyard, so the device can be worn around the neck and is readily to hand.

Despite providing an ingenious solution to a recurrent problem, Charlie's dispenser has not yet made it into production. However, the two leading manufacturers, Carmex and ChapStick, have stated they would like to develop new applicators that are easier to use, so it is just possible they might draw upon Charlie's design.

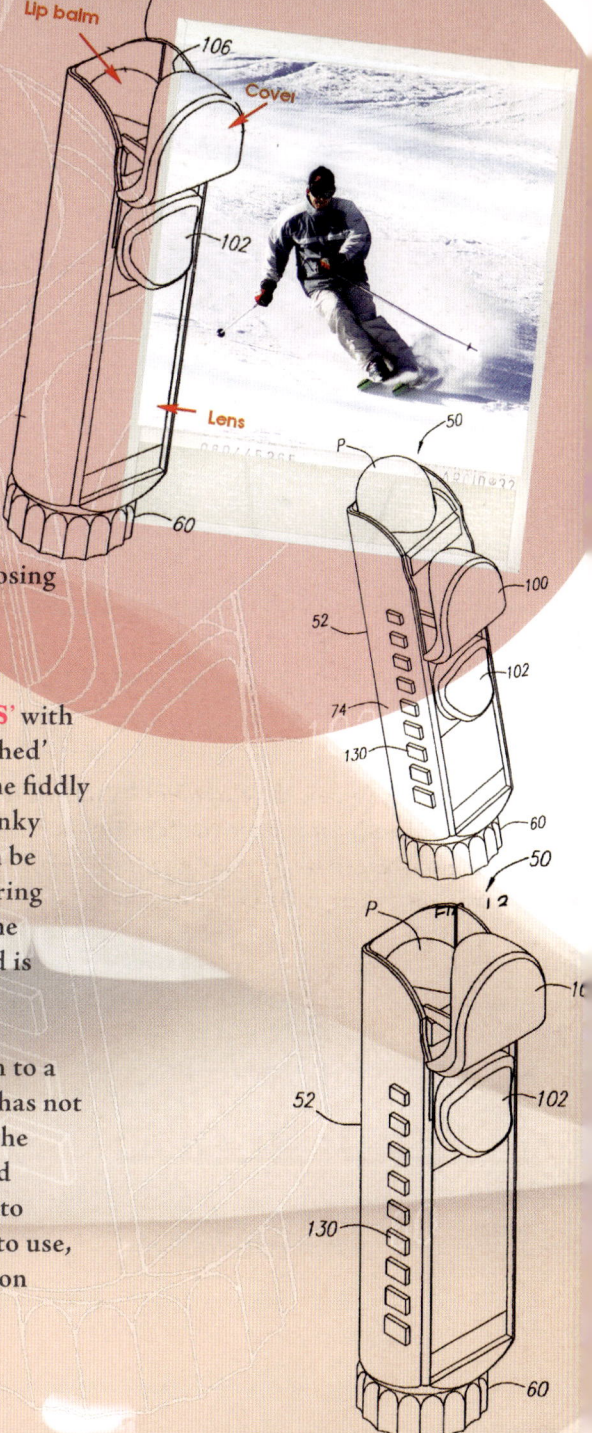

PUTTING A SHEEN ON THINGS

In 2005 Charlie turned his hand to fashion design and launched a range of children's clothing called 'Sheen Kidz', which he says was inspired by his daughters Sam and Lola. Aiming to be 'practical and beautiful, sturdy but stylish', **THE BRAND REPORTEDLY SOLD OVER $15 MILLION OF CLOTHING IN ITS FIRST SEASON OF OPERATION**, despite being somewhat at odds with Charlie Sheen's 'bad-boy' persona.

Perhaps more in line with his reputation, in the last year **HE HAS LENT HIS NAME TO A NEW E-CIGARETTE, BRANDED AS THE 'NICO-SHEEN'.** The smokeless 'electronic cigarette' dispenses nicotine and its packaging includes Charlie's signature and grinning face. It's still early days for the gadget, but Charlie is doing his best to publicize it, ensuring that he has been photographed on stage and in the street puffing on the novelty device.

RECORD-BREAKING MONEY TALK

In early 2011 Charlie went through a very public breakdown and his behaviour in the social media space – such as Twitter and Facebook – became still more unpredictable. As a result, Charlie set a new Guinness World Record as the 'Fastest Time to Reach 1 Million Twitter Followers'. **HE ADDED AN AVERAGE OF 129,000 NEW FOLLOWERS PER DAY,** and has since been hired by dozens of companies to promote their products in his tweets.

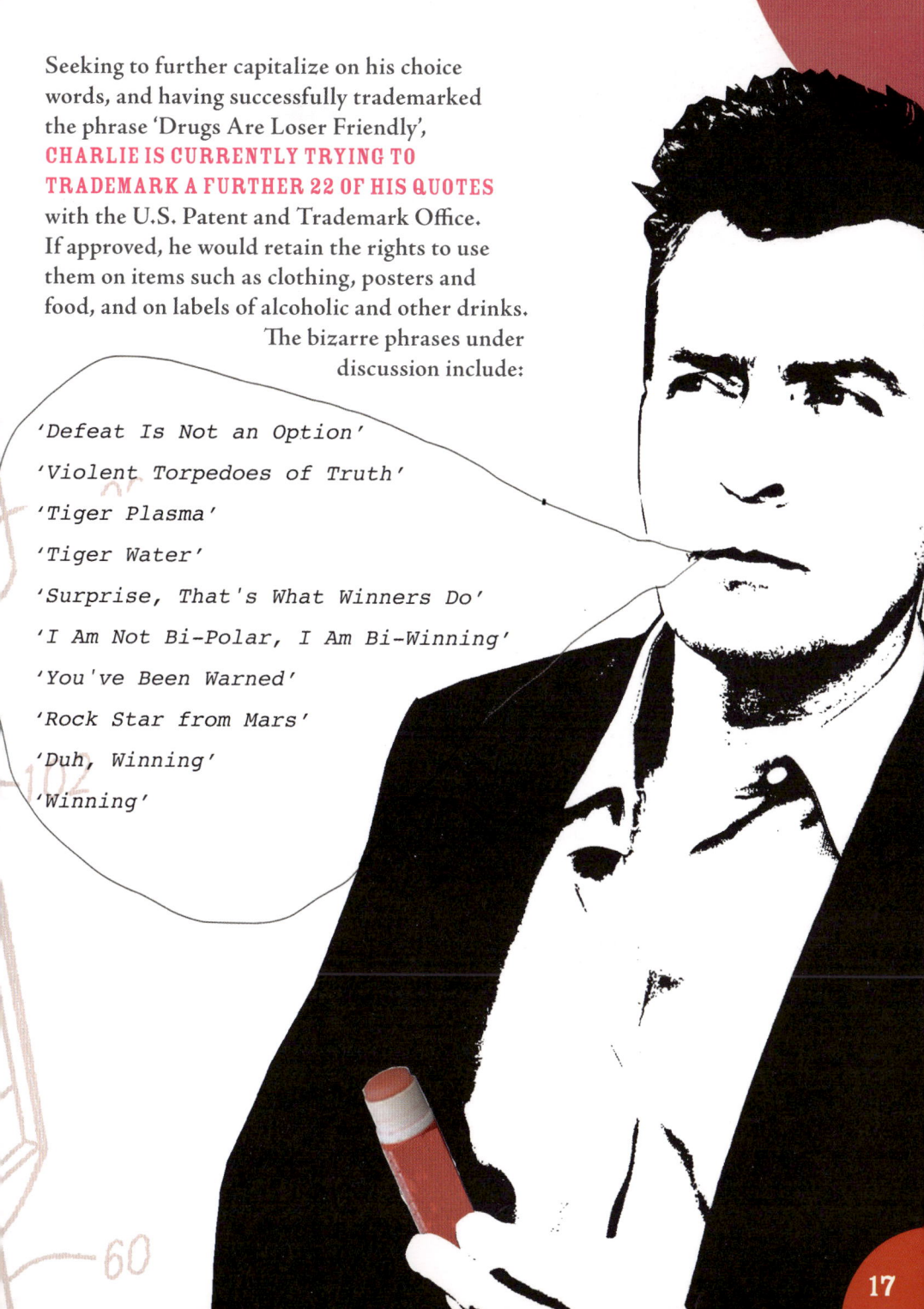

Seeking to further capitalize on his choice words, and having successfully trademarked the phrase 'Drugs Are Loser Friendly', **CHARLIE IS CURRENTLY TRYING TO TRADEMARK A FURTHER 22 OF HIS QUOTES** with the U.S. Patent and Trademark Office. If approved, he would retain the rights to use them on items such as clothing, posters and food, and on labels of alcoholic and other drinks. The bizarre phrases under discussion include:

'Defeat Is Not an Option'
'Violent Torpedoes of Truth'
'Tiger Plasma'
'Tiger Water'
'Surprise, That's What Winners Do'
'I Am Not Bi-Polar, I Am Bi-Winning'
'You've Been Warned'
'Rock Star from Mars'
'Duh, Winning'
'Winning'

STEVE McQUEEN

THE McQUEEN RACING SEAT

STEVE MCQUEEN, AMERICAN ACTOR AND UNDISPUTED KING OF COOL, STARRED IN ACTION FILMS FOR DECADES, COMPLETING EVER-MORE DEATH-DEFYING FEATS AS HIS CAREER WENT ON. HE WAS SOMETHING OF AN ADRENALINE JUNKIE, ESPECIALLY WHEN IT CAME TO CARS, AND THIS INSPIRED A CLEVER AUTOMOTIVE INVENTION.

Steve funded his acting training through his winnings in motorcycle races, so when he was offered the opportunity to drive in a movie, he jumped at the chance to draw on his expertise.

During the high-speed chase scene in the film *Bullitt*, **STEVE WAS REQUIRED TO DRIVE THROUGH THE HILLY STREETS AND TIGHT BENDS OF SAN FRANCISCO AT SPEEDS IN EXCESS OF 100MPH.** Since the driving was so demanding, he requested a number of changes be made to his (now infamous) Ford Mustang Fastback. He had the engine

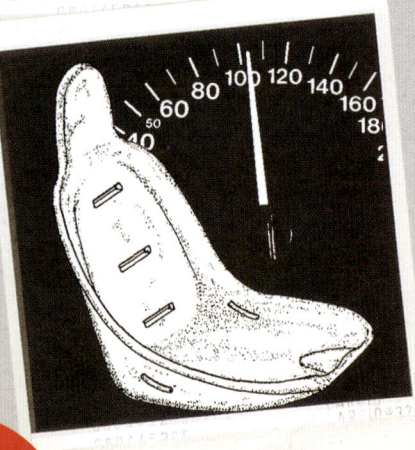

tuned to provide more power, stiffened the suspension and made modifications to the driving seat. Out went the spongy production seat, and in its place **HE DESIGNED A MONOCOQUE 'ONE-PIECE' RACING SEAT.** He also specifically designed a figure-hugging shape to fit him perfectly and support the sides of his body when cornering.

Steve also modified the seat belts, which dug into him as he rounded the tight corners of San Francisco. To remedy this he moved the belt points and installed racing straps to hold him securely in place.

These alterations allowed him to drive solidly for the three weeks it took to shoot the film's chase scenes. Although the crew started with two cars, the driving was so extreme that in the process of filming one of these was written off. **BUT THROUGHOUT THE FILMING SCHEDULE STEVE'S SEAT REMAINED INTACT.** In fact, he was so pleased with the design that in he filed a patent for it in 1971.

After the filming of *Bullitt*, Steve insisted that his seat was fitted in every car he drove in subsequent movies, and he even used it for motor racing. While filming the movie *Le Mans*, Steve was given the actual car that had driven in the famous 24-hour race. He negotiated at length with the manufacturer, Porsche, to gain their permission to have his seat fitted – and won.

FANS IN THE HOT SEAT

Steve McQueen's patent expired over ten years ago. The design was never commercialized, and the original bucket seat he used has been lost. However, using the details filed at the US patent office, **STEVE'S FANS HAVE BEEN RE-CREATING THEIR VERY OWN STEVE MCQUEEN RACING SEATS AND FITTING THEM IN THEIR CARS.** The seat itself is reportedly tremendously comfortable, with the added benefit of enabling the driver to experience a little of the McQueen cool. However, a number of fans have also confessed to having received speeding tickets since installing their go-faster seats.

THE MYSTERY OF THE MISSING MUSTANG

The whereabouts of the surviving car used in *Bullitt* is currently unknown. It was initially sold to an employee of Warner Brothers' editing department, but the car then changed hands several times, and at one point even Steve McQueen made an unsuccessful attempt to buy it. **CURRENTLY ESTIMATED TO BE WORTH OVER TEN MILLION DOLLARS**, the lost Mustang is rumoured to be stashed somewhere in the Ohio River Valley by an anonymous owner.

HARRY HILL

HARRY'S NUTS

AWARD-WINNING COMEDIAN HARRY HILL IS THE INFAMOUS PRESENTER OF ITV'S *YOU'VE BEEN FRAMED* AND *HARRY HILL'S TV BURP*. A FAN OF BIG COLLARS AND HEAVY 'BAT-WING' GLASSES, HE ACTUALLY STARTED OUT HIS CAREER AS A MEDICAL DOCTOR – IN FACT, HE IS STILL A REGISTERED PRACTITIONER. HARRY BECAME INTERESTED IN COMEDY IN THE EARLY NINETIES AND NEVER LOOKED BACK – WHICH HAS DONE THE WORLD A FAVOUR AS HE NOW USES HIS CELEBRITY STATUS TO HELP THE LESS FORTUNATE.

Harry is a long-term supporter of Fairtrade, which provided the inspiration behind his very own snack range: **'HARRY'S NUTS!'** Harry launched the product after travelling to Africa and meeting some of the peanut farmers, many of whom were women looking after Aids orphans.

' I have invented my own nuts! I love salted peanuts and feel I am doing a service to snackers everywhere who want to know that the farmers who grew what they are eating have been paid fairly.

So, I've teamed up with a company that is solely run to benefit the farmers and their families.

There's no money in it for me – what a mug! The idea is that because the farmers are paid a fair price, they are directly able to improve their own lives.

I went to Africa to see the results a few years ago and saw that Fairtrade really works.

You can find my nuts in all good supermarkets, and I can guarantee satisfaction. They are very tasty.'

At the heart of the project is the desire to see farmers being paid fairly for their crops, and it is clear that from both of Harry's career choices that he is motivated by making people happy, gladly using his name to promote projects that do good.

A TASTE OF SUCCESS

Harry's Nuts were launched in 2009 and are proving extremely popular. The extra funds raised by the farmers have been used to establish better storage facilities to help keep the nuts in top condition before being exported; it's thought the stores will also be used to keep essential items such as mosquito nets for families and seed for farmers who have lost their crops.

Money has also gone towards building a shelter for the relatives of hospital patients so they don't have to sleep out in the open, and grants have paid for shelling machines that automate the slow, boring work previously done by hand.

Buoyed by the success of this idea, Harry is now pushing sales of his new peanut butter.

D'YOU KNOW WHAT THEY SHOULD MAKE…?

Harry is not alone in lending his name to a food range. Celebrity chefs such as Jamie Oliver and Gordon Ramsay sell their own cooking sauces, actor Paul Newman created a range of salad dressing, and sports people and singers such as David Beckham and Beyoncé have used their names to promote fizzy drinks. Here are some celebrity confectionery endorsements just waiting to happen.

Amy Wine-Gums
Andy Murray Mints
Ringo Starrburst
Cheryl Cola Bottles
The Duchess of Yorkie Bar
Jon Bon-Bon Jovi

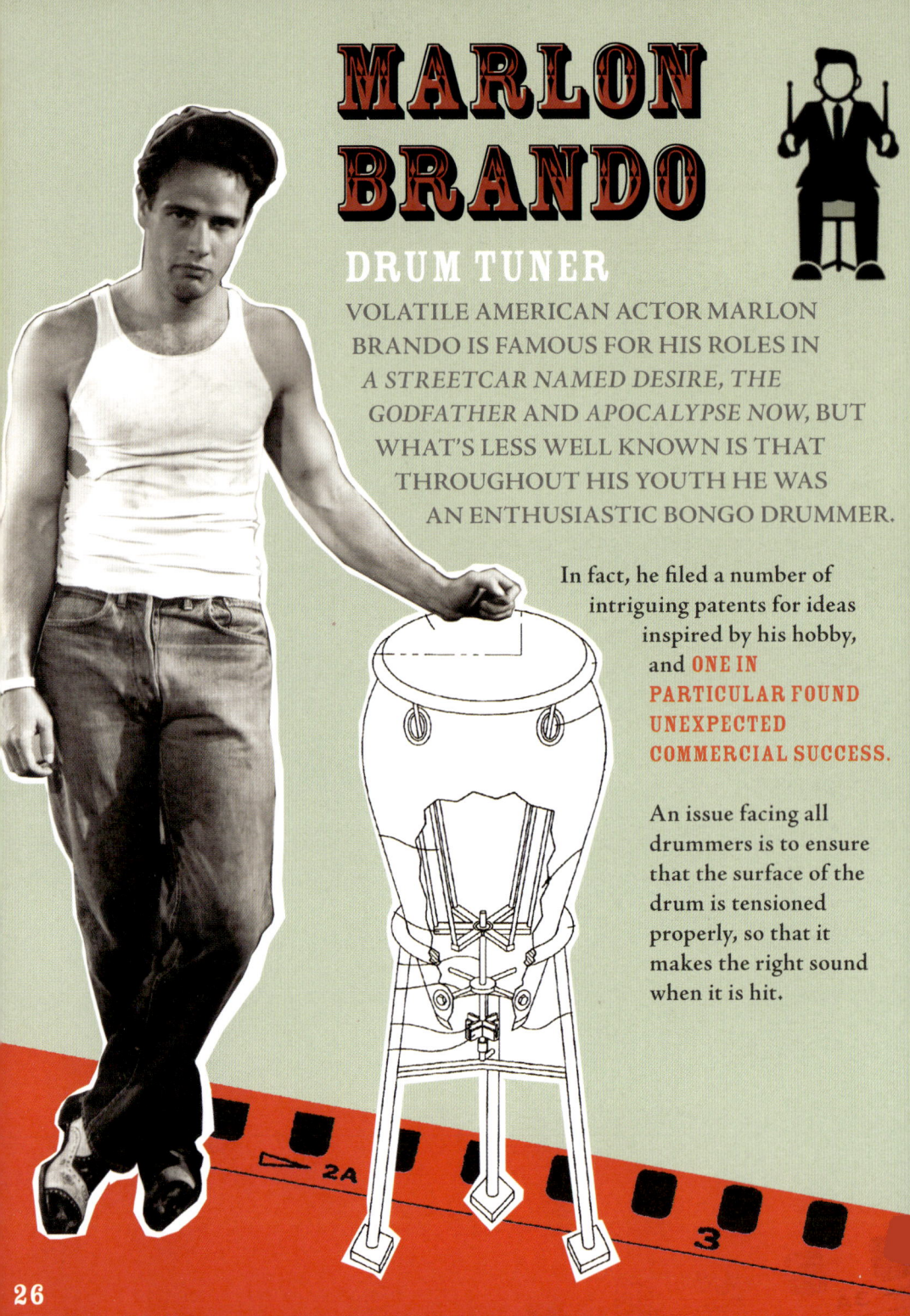

Like any instrument, a drum needs to be tuned, but due to the nature of the instrument this is harder than you might think. The playing surface is stretched and held at four different points, so tightening the tension at just one point doesn't work. The whole surface needs to be pulled tight so that the tension is uniform across the skin, achieving the best timbre. This is quite a time-consuming task, and more than a little tricky.

So **MARLON DEVISED AN INGENIOUS MECHANISED SOLUTION:** he invented a system that pulls each of the four tensioning points at the same time. The system is electronic, so that the whole drum surface can be uniformly tensioned or slackened at the touch of a button.

He even incorporated an automatic tuning device in the invention. As the drum surface is being tightened it can be tested by the musician: tapping it creates a string of notes, the pitch of which gets progressively higher. When the right note is struck, the tuner automatically holds the tension, leaving the drum perfectly tuned.

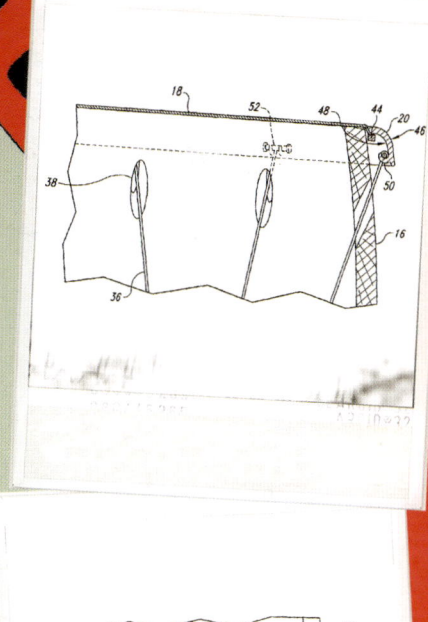

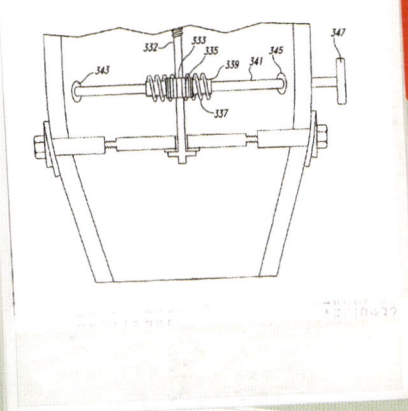

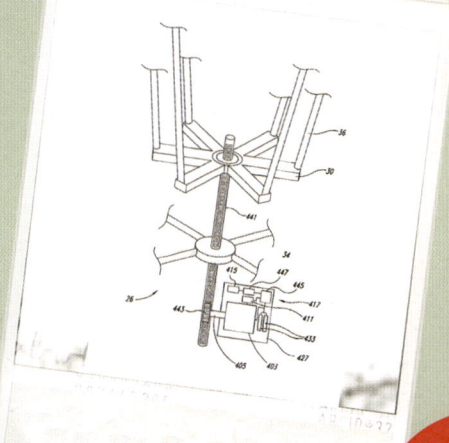

The whole invention is cleverly located inside the drum, so you would never know it was there!

BANGING THE DRUM

In 2002, when he filed his invention, Marlon was 76 years old and had withdrawn from the public eye. Throughout his career he had been notoriously difficult to work with: he was quick to anger, often unwilling to memorize lines, resistant to direction and, whilst making *The Godfather*, he even skipped the last day of filming.

Marlon was also fined $4,000 for punching a photographer, who subsequently took to wearing an American football helmet whenever he photographed him.

For Marlon, playing the drums was a way to relax and unwind, and he said that it was in this state that he was best able to find inspiration and generate ideas. In an interview late in his life he described how ideas such as this invention simply 'popped into his head' whilst he was drumming.

PLAYING TO A DIFFERENT TUNE

Marlon's drum-tuning invention turned into a lucrative idea and found its way into many products from leading drum manufacturers. Marlon regularly joked that the only reason he was in Hollywood was that he didn't have the moral courage to refuse the money, so it's ironic that if he had indulged his drumming a little more and patented the idea earlier, he might never have needed to be in Hollywood at all.

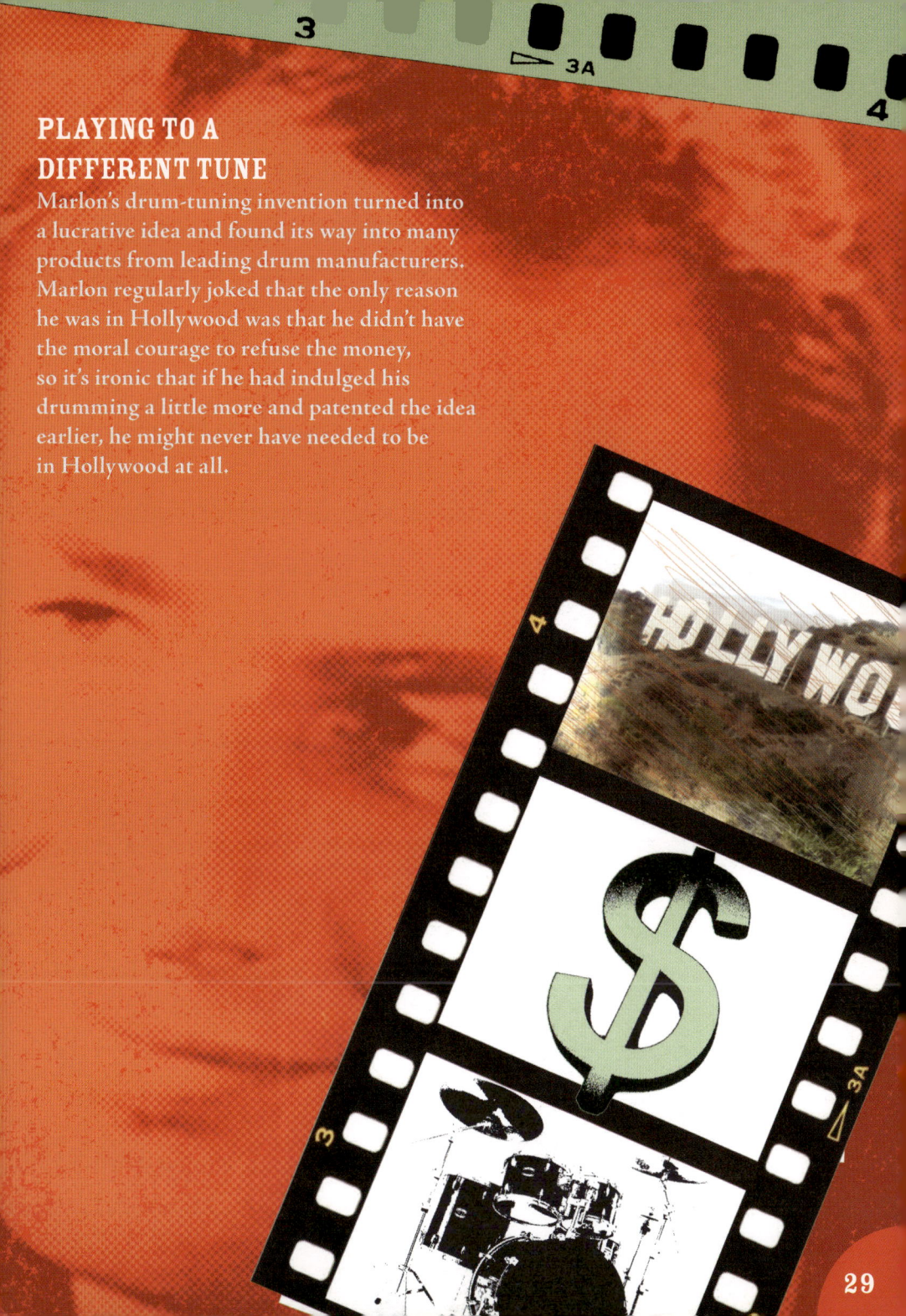

RUBY WAX

THE 'ULTIMATE BAG WOMAN' BAGS

COMEDIENNE EXTRAORDINAIRE RUBY WAX MADE HER NAME AS A COMEDIC ACTOR AND UNINHIBITED INTERVIEWER OF HIGH-PROFILE PUBLIC FIGURES, FROM THE DUCHESS OF YORK TO O.J. SIMPSON.

Motivated by a recurrent problem in her life, **IN 2005 SHE TURNED HER HAND TO INVENTING**, and in 2010 even appeared on TV's *Dragons' Den* to pitch a new product idea.

BECAUSE SHE COULDN'T FIND ANYTHING IN HER BAGS SHE DECIDED TO CREATE A RANGE OF TRANSPARENT TRAVEL BAGS, which let you find everything you need without having to empty the contents out onto the floor.

Called the 'The Ultimate Bag Woman' bags, they are made from tough, see-through waterproof plastic so you can easily see what is inside, but they won't fall apart.

There are five designs with different names, covered in graffiti-style lipstick-red slogans. 'Tart Art' is for your make-up, 'Hang Ups' is a holiday pouch with two separate compartments for your clean and dirty underwear. 'On Your Face' is a wash bag, with separate sections for soaps, creams and brushes, and sealed pockets for all the bits you don't want people to see.

Designed to be a send-up of fashion, Ruby credits creating them because there isn't anything like them out there, claiming that, having made them, she can't go anywhere without them!

A CLEAR SUCCESS

Ruby's transparent bags echo her transparent approach to interviewing celebrities and talking about herself. She has spoken honestly about the twists in her life and has even taken to the stage with a confessional cabaret show detailing the highs and lows of her career. It's called 'Losing It'.

THE BAGS WERE OPPORTUNELY RELEASED JUST AS SECURITY MEASURES IN AIRPORTS WERE STEPPED UP, making it mandatory to place toiletries in transparent bags. Her invention not only made the lives of security officers easier, but also provided a stylish and durable solution for travellers.

The range was snapped up quickly by consumers and sold in high-street chain Boots for a number of years; it still sees significant orders online today. **EVEN PRADA AND CHANEL GOT IN ON THE ACT,** releasing their own sets of transparent handbags and luggage.

HARD TIMES FOR THE BOOTY BUSTER

Unafraid to show more of her entrepreneural side, Ruby used her experience launching her own product range to support two businesswomen as they entered the *Dragons' Den*.

In a special edition of the programme, which raised funds for Sport Relief, she appeared with two inventors demonstrating their new home fitness idea, the **'BOOTY BUSTER'**. Using her experience of bringing her bags to the market, Ruby assisted with the presentation by demonstrating the product and creating a compelling story about how it could be used.

Unfortunately, despite her best efforts, the invention didn't win any investment. Why was this? **'BUSINESS IS CRUEL'**, she explained afterwards.

JAMIE LEE CURTIS

WET WIPE NAPPY

ACTRESS JAMIE LEE CURTIS STARRED IN A STRING OF HOLLYWOOD BLOCKBUSTERS, INCLUDING *A FISH CALLED WANDA*, *TRUE LIES* AND THE HORROR MOVIE *HALLOWEEN*. SHE IS MARRIED TO COMIC ACTOR CHRISTOPHER GUEST AND IS MOTHER TO TWO CHILDREN, AND IT THIS LATTER ROLE THAT INSPIRED HER HANDY INVENTION.

Having partially suspended her acting career in the late eighties to bring up two young children, Jamie Lee became absorbed in the everyday trials and tribulations of childcare. One particular babycare task alerted her to an opportunity for innovation, and so in 1987 she filed a patent for the WET WIPE NAPPY.

It's not often that you hear a famous Hollywood actress talk about her nappy-changing experiences, so JAMIE LEE'S PATENT DOCUMENT IS A RARE BEHIND-THE-SCENES-GLIMPSE OF A CELEBRITY'S DOMESTIC LIFE.

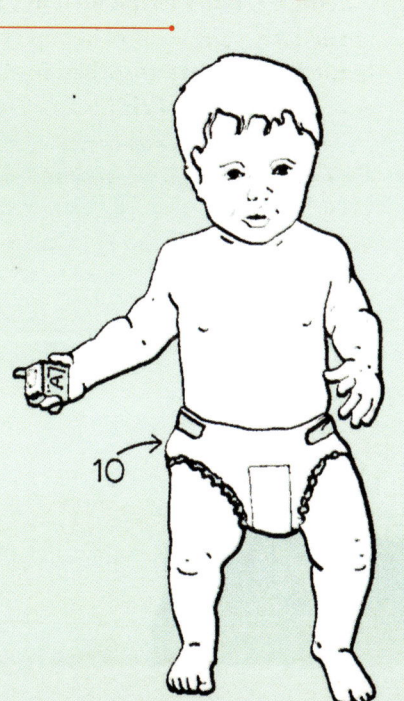

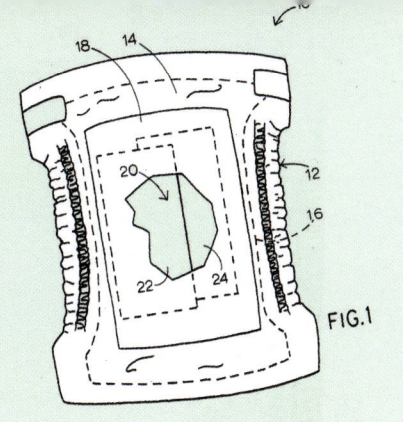

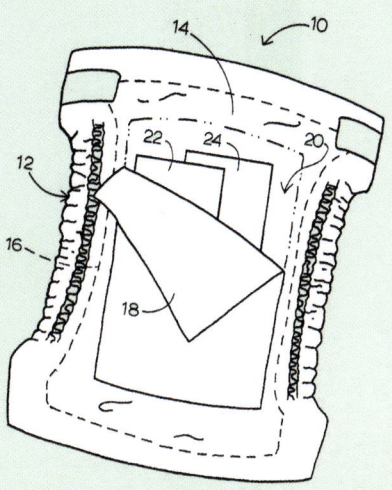

FIG.1

FIG.2

> **Parents everywhere are all too familiar with the trials of nappy changing and having to juggle soiled and clean nappies and necessary baby-care products while trying to calm the infant at the same time. While the introduction of disposable nappies and moisturised cleaning wipes has gone a long way to simplifying the process, there is still room for improvement. The solution? The Wet Wipe Nappy.**

FIG.3

The invention Jamie Lee proposed was for a nappy that incorporates a sealed pocket on the outside that can be filled with wet wipes. This means the wipes will be readily available and in close proximity to where they are required, so parents can hold the nappy and remove the wipes using only one hand. Combining wipes and nappy also eliminates the need to store, dispense and travel with two separately packaged items.

THE NUISANCE OF NAPPIES

Although Jamie Lee's design provides a smart solution to a potentially sticky situation, and helps make parents' lives that little bit easier, after patenting her design JAMIE LEE BEGAN TO HAVE CONCERNS ABOUT THE ENVIRONMENTAL IMPLICATIONS OF HER IDEA.

She worried that the average kid will probably go through hundreds of nappies as they grow up, so there's likely to be billions of nappies used every year.

The disposable nappies she used take hundreds of years to degrade and can contain all kinds of nasty glues and plastics.

As a consequence she expressed that, environmentally, she would be like a slum lord, making something that ultimately would pollute the Earth with landfill. So she decided not to let anyone use the design until biodegradable, environmental nappies can be made.

A Nappy Ending...

The good news is that new biodegradable disposable nappies are just beginning to be introduced to the market. A company called Moltex is leading the way, and could be a prime candidate for collaboration with Jamie Lee. So, the Wet Wipe Nappy may yet come to the rescue of parents everywhere.

PAUL NEWMAN

'NEWMAN'S OWN' FOOD RANGE

PAUL NEWMAN WAS A HUGELY SUCCESSFUL AMERICAN ACTOR, PROBABLY BEST KNOWN FOR FILMS SUCH AS *BUTCH CASSIDY AND THE SUNDANCE KID*, *THE COLOR OF MONEY*, AND *THE STING*. ALONGSIDE HIS ACTING, THOUGH, PAUL WAS AN ENTREPRENEUR, PHILANTHROPIST AND KEEN COOK, AND IT WAS THIS COMBINATION OF THESE INTERESTS THAT LED PAUL TO INVENT HIS OWN FOOD RANGE.

The 'Newman's Own' brand started with a home-made salad dressing that Paul and his friend, author Aaron Hotchner, used to make and give away to friends. They made it because neither of them liked the taste and artificial ingredients of shop-bought dressings, so they set up making limited amounts of their own recipe in Paul's barn.

The dressing went down so well that the pair decided to make and sell it in larger quantities, and donate the profits to charity. In 1982, using $40,000 of Paul's money, they started manufacturing the sauce. The first proper bottle label incorporated a smiling picture of Paul and the strapline: **'NEWMAN'S OWN SALAD DRESSING, FINE FOODS SINCE FEBRUARY.'**

The dressing proved a huge success, and soon Paul and Aaron expanded their range to include sauces, marinades, cereal, pizzas, lemonade, popcorn and wine.

True to his word, **PAUL DONATED 100% OF THE PROFITS TO GOOD CAUSES**, and in a typically offbeat statement he confirmed:

> *All the profits will be divided between a number of tax-deductible charities and causes, some church-related, others for conservation and ecology and things like that.*

Paul had always been an active campaigner for the environment, equal rights and the peace movement (for his outspoken opposition to the war in Vietnam, Newman was placed 19th on Richard Nixon's enemies list, which he said was his greatest accomplishment), and so as the brand grew, Paul set up a number of his own charities to reflect those causes that most strongly concerned him. He also established a foundation to distribute the money.

One such charity is the **'HOLE IN THE WALL'** camps. These residential summer camps for seriously ill children were co-founded by Paul and a business partner in 1988. Today, there are **11 MEMBER CAMPS AROUND THE WORLD**, with additional programs in Africa and Vietnam. To date, over 135,000 children have attended the camps free of charge.

Paul and Aaron co-wrote a memoir of their experiences setting up Newman's Own, entitled **THE SHAMELESS EXPLOITATION IN PURSUIT OF THE COMMON GOOD,** in which they explain the success of the brand:

> Newman's Own was supposed to be a tiny boutique operation, putting parchment labels on elegant wine bottles made of antique glass. We expected train wrecks along the way and got instead, one astonishment after another. We flourished like weeds in a garden, like silver in the vaults of finance. We anticipated sales of $1,200 a year and a loss, but since we started we have earned over $300 million, which we've given to countless charities. How to account for this massive success? Pure luck? Transcendental meditation? Machiavellian manipulation? Aerodynamics? High colonics? We haven't the slightest idea.

Paul's comment on the brand was:

> The embarrassing thing is that the salad dressing is outgrossing my films.

And when asked about his philanthropy, he simply stated:

> You can only put so much stuff in your closet.

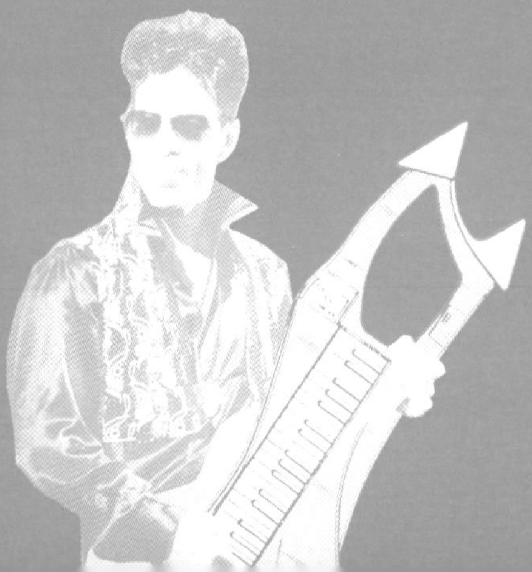

2. MUSICIANS & DIRECTORS

MICHAEL JACKSON

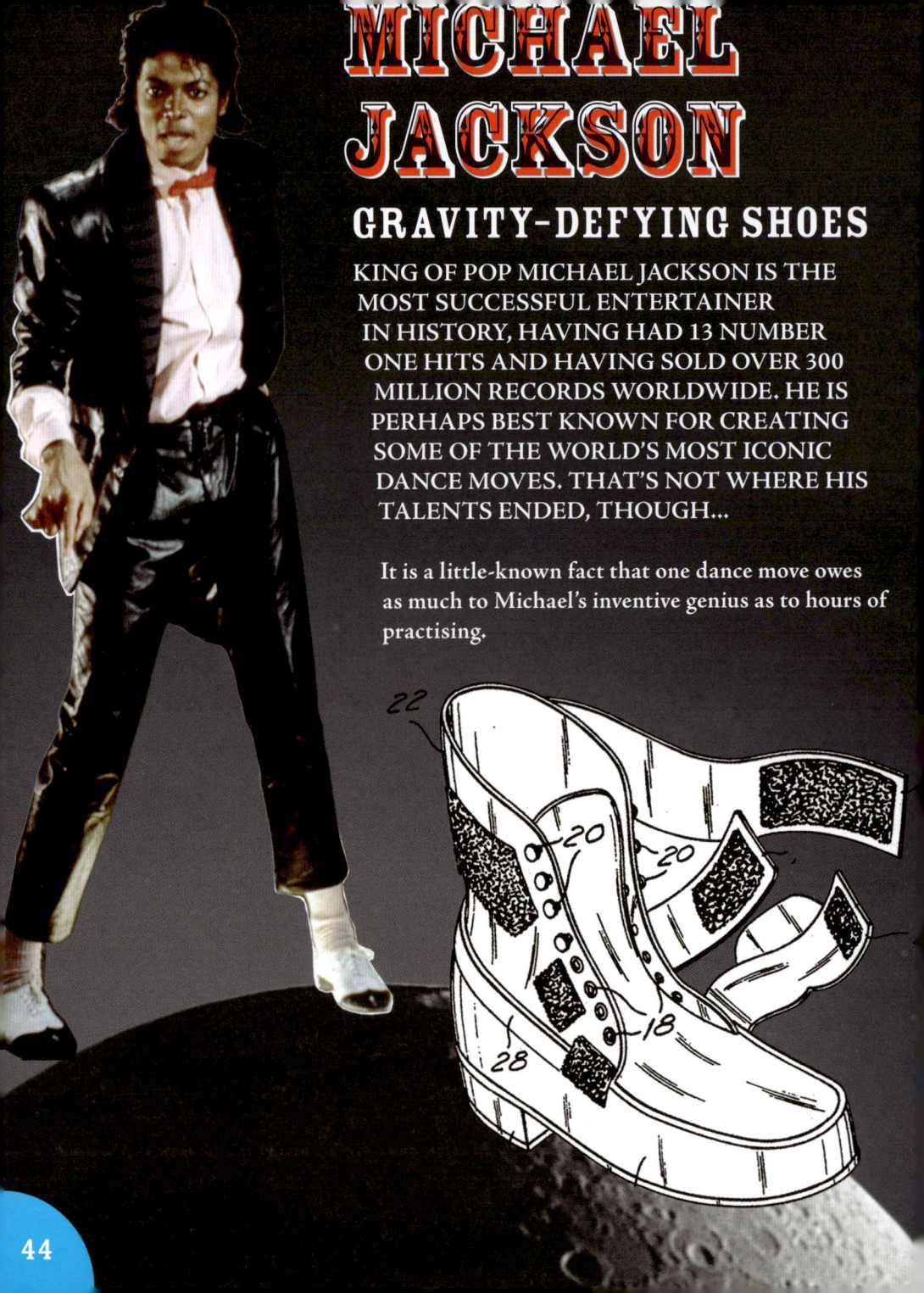

GRAVITY-DEFYING SHOES

KING OF POP MICHAEL JACKSON IS THE MOST SUCCESSFUL ENTERTAINER IN HISTORY, HAVING HAD 13 NUMBER ONE HITS AND HAVING SOLD OVER 300 MILLION RECORDS WORLDWIDE. HE IS PERHAPS BEST KNOWN FOR CREATING SOME OF THE WORLD'S MOST ICONIC DANCE MOVES. THAT'S NOT WHERE HIS TALENTS ENDED, THOUGH…

It is a little-known fact that one dance move owes as much to Michael's inventive genius as to hours of practising.

You can see this particular 'move' at work in the video for his multi-million-selling single 'Smooth Criminal'. **MICHAEL LEANS FORWARD AT A GRAVITY-DEFYING 45-DEGREE ANGLE** – well past the physical limits of standing up. This would be completely out of the question without a pair of cleverly made shoes designed by Michael himself.

Michael's live shows made use of the shoe design constantly. During performances of 'Smooth Criminal', a set of mushroom-shaped 'hitches' pop up from the stage beneath the dancers' feet. They then shuffle forward, engaging a slot in the heel of their shoe over the head of the mushroom-shaped hitch and wedging the shoe in place.

THE DANCERS ARE THEN FIXED TO THE STAGE, AS IF SOMEONE WERE HOLDING DOWN THE BACKS OF THEIR SHOES, enabling them to lean over beyond the point at which they would normally fall. After the move, the dancers shuffle backwards, disengaging the hitch, which would be lowered back into the stage.

In 1993 Michael filed a patent for this nifty footwear design.

45

DID THE SHOE FIT?

Michael's footwear has been used in hundreds of performances and has wowed audiences all over the world. However, it is possible to catch Michael's trick in action, as **FOOTAGE OF LIVE PERFORMANCES OF 'SMOOTH CRIMINAL' OCCASIONALLY REVEAL THE ODD SLIP-UP,** when dancers attempt to perform the manoeuvre and momentarily get wedged in place on stage, unable to disengage their shoes from the hitch for a few seonds.

A STEP FURTHER

After his death in 2009, **MANY OF MICHAEL'S FANS TOOK A NOSTALGIC LOOK AT HIS GRAVITY-DEFYING FOOTWEAR,** with some even suggesting ideas to take his invention one step further.

Inspired by a Victorian petty-thief named 'Spring-Heeled Jack', comedian Nick Thune had the idea to develop the footwear to enable dancers to do an instantaneous backflip. Spring-Heeled Jack was said to stalk the streets of London wearing shoes with spring heels that enabled him to rob people then make off at high speed, leaping over obstacles too high for anyone to follow. Nick's concept takes the idea one stage further, suggesting that **POWERFUL COILED SPRINGS ARE FITTED UNDER THE FRONT OF A PAIR OF SHOES.** In his version, when the wearer presses a button the springs activate and the wearer does a backflip. Or, as he puts it: **'THE SHOES DO THE BACKFLIP AND THE WEARER COMES ALONG FOR THE RIDE.'**

One other idea put forward by a US inventor was that Michael's shoes could be adapted **SO THEY WOULD SQUIRT BUBBLES FROM THE HEEL.** A soapy solution would be poured into a cavity in the sole, then the action of dancing would push air through the underside of the shoe to create the bubbles.

JAMES CAMERON

UNDERWATER VEHICLE FOR 3D FILMING

JAMES CAMERON IS ONE OF THE MOST SUCCESSFUL BIG-BUDGET FILM DIRECTORS OF ALL TIME. HE STARTED OUT IN THE 1980S WITH HITS SUCH AS *THE TERMINATOR*, *THE ABYSS* AND *ALIENS*, THEN WENT ON TO MAKE TWO OF THE HIGHEST-GROSSING BLOCKBUSTERS OF ALL TIME, *TITANIC* AND *AVATAR*.

A fan of science and innovation, James has been responsible for developing some of the most sophisticated technology for filming in 3D, and recently patented a remarkable aquatic invention that aims to revolutionize underwater filming.

The son of an electrical engineer, James studied physics at college and was so inspired after watching *Star Wars* that he quit his job to pursue a career in the film industry. **HE HAS BECOME A MAJOR INFUENCE IN FILMMAKING EVER SINCE,** wowing audiences with cutting-edge special effects.

He also has developed a speciality in making spectacular underwater movies. After directing *Titanic*, James was inspired by the idea of exploring inaccessible shipwrecks, and took on a project to make a documentary film. It concerned the wreck of a sunken Second World War German battleship, the *Bismarck*, which lies 600 miles west of France at the bottom of the Atlantic Ocean. The wreck is nearly 5,000 metres below sea level, so filming the ship provided significant technical challenges, meaning **JAMES BECAME FAMILIAR WITH CUTTING-EDGE UNDERWATER CAMERA EQUIPMENT.**

Hungry for more underwater action, James was approached by Disney to make a similar feature-length documentary about exploring the wreck of the *Titanic* – this time in 3D. In order to capture the 3D footage, James and his team developed the Fusion 3D Camera System, a groundbreaking new way to film 3D scenes. However, the cumbersome fusion camera is extremely hard to propel and manoeuvre under water. Consequently, James drew on his knowledge of the latest undersea equipment and his background in physics to develop an innovative solution.

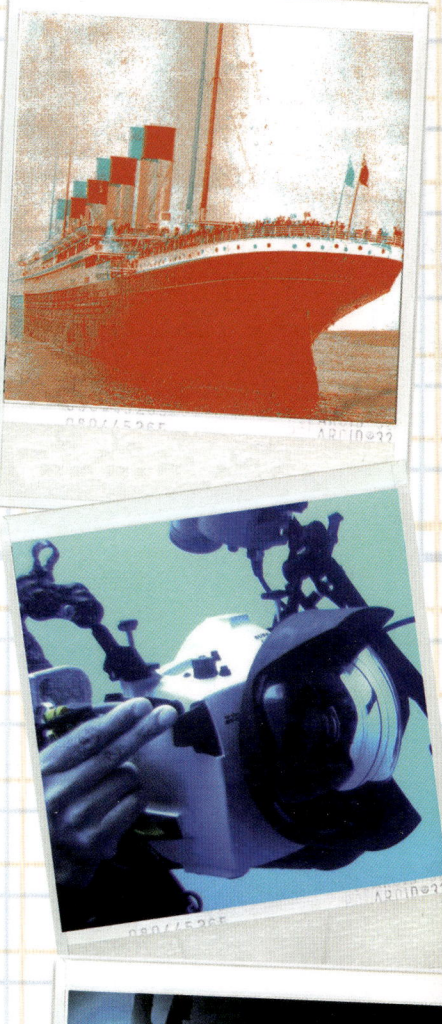

James invented **A SMART PROPULSION SYSTEM THAT ALLOWS A CAMERA OPERATOR TO MOVE EFFORTLESSLY THROUGH THE WATER** while filming their surroundings – it is essentially an underwater vehicle with two thrusters that can propel both a diver and the fusion camera. The key innovation allows the camera to be swivelled and pointed wherever required, independent of the direction in which the vehicle is travelling. The resultant documentary, *Ghosts of the Abyss*, made extensive use of James's underwater vehicle and proved extremely successful. James's most recent project, *The Dive*, once again made use of his underwater vehicle to propel the camera, and his invention is likely to find wider applications for divers across the world.

THREE-DIMENSIONAL SUCCESS

The 3D Fusion Camera developed for *Ghosts of the Abyss* was later used to create the spectacular 3D effects in *Avatar*.

In 2010, *Avatar* became the highest-grossing film in history, taking almost $2 billion at the box office. Following its success, James Cameron announced all his films would now be made in 3D. Until now, 3D films have used a range of techniques, most of which entail viewers wearing glasses; the principle behind these techniques is to show each eye a slightly different image, which creates the illusion of depth.

In the 1970s 'Anaglyph' glasses were pioneered, which use a red filter on one eye and blue on the other. The next major development was the use of polarized glasses, which work on the same principle but use polarizing filters rather than coloured ones. This technique is used in *Ghosts of the Abyss* and *Avatar*.

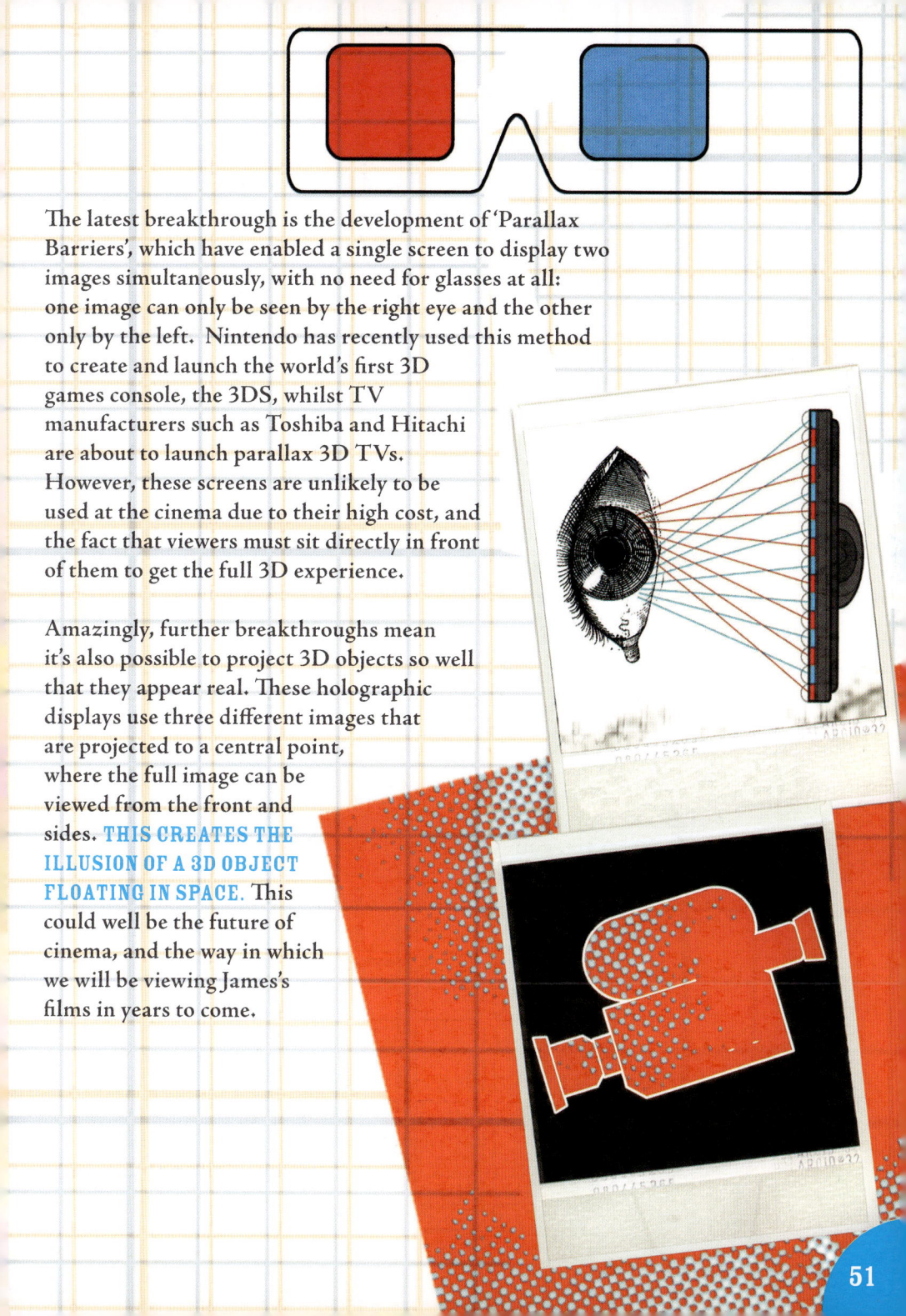

The latest breakthrough is the development of 'Parallax Barriers', which have enabled a single screen to display two images simultaneously, with no need for glasses at all: one image can only be seen by the right eye and the other only by the left. Nintendo has recently used this method to create and launch the world's first 3D games console, the 3DS, whilst TV manufacturers such as Toshiba and Hitachi are about to launch parallax 3D TVs. However, these screens are unlikely to be used at the cinema due to their high cost, and the fact that viewers must sit directly in front of them to get the full 3D experience.

Amazingly, further breakthroughs mean it's also possible to project 3D objects so well that they appear real. These holographic displays use three different images that are projected to a central point, where the full image can be viewed from the front and sides. **THIS CREATES THE ILLUSION OF A 3D OBJECT FLOATING IN SPACE.** This could well be the future of cinema, and the way in which we will be viewing James's films in years to come.

NICOLA ROBERTS

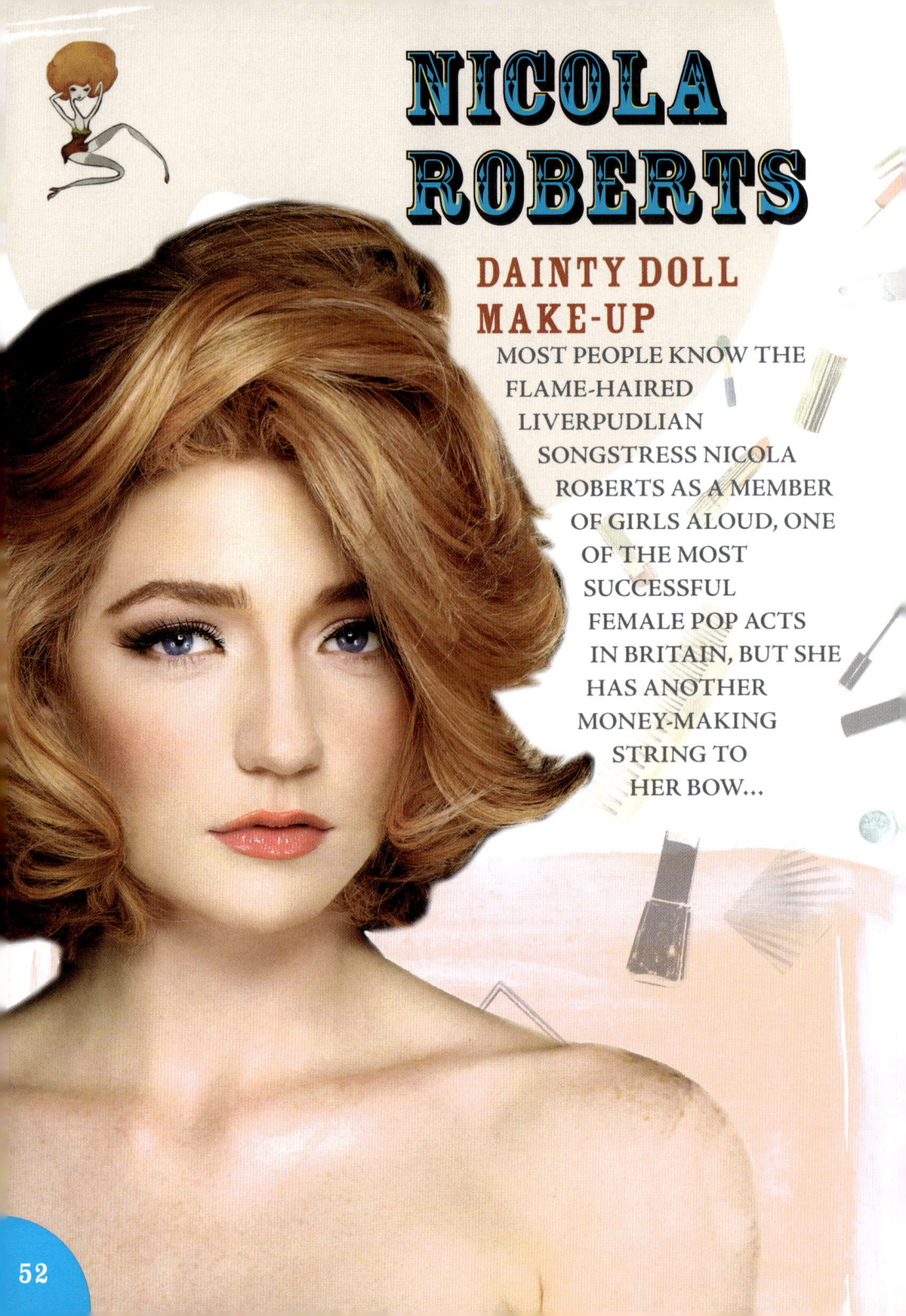

DAINTY DOLL MAKE-UP

Most people know the flame-haired Liverpudlian songstress Nicola Roberts as a member of Girls Aloud, one of the most successful female pop acts in Britain, but she has another money-making string to her bow…

52

From the moment Nicola won a place in the band after competing in TV talent show *Popstars: The Rivals,* her life was turned upside down. In her first years in the limelight **NICOLA CONFESSED TO BEING INSECURE ABOUT HER LOOKS AND PALE COMPLEXION,** but she later overcame this and went on to invent a product that would help other pale-skinned women do the same.

' I feel very proud to have created a make-up line for women who, like myself, have pale skin. It's called Dainty Doll. I'm really passionate about the range, and I worked very closely with the chemists and illustrators on perfecting formulations, colours and graphics. Every detail needs to be perfect.

I want Dainty Doll not only to suit women but to also help them. Like many I have suffered with problem skin, so I know what it feels like to want to cover up and at the same time feel guilty about layering on chemically-enriched foundations. I decided my range should have a natural formula, so there is no more need for that guilt. My concealers even have an anti-inflammatory ingredient to reduce redness and swelling throughout the day.

I hope my invention will make a difference to other women and help them learn to love their beautiful skin. '

Nicola's innovation offers a contrast to the tan-obsessed make-up industry of the twenty-first century, and **DAINTY DOLL IS SELLING WELL ACROSS THE COUNTRY**, from Harrods to asos.com. As an advocate of banning sunbed usage for minors and a passionate supporter of natural beauty, **NICOLA HAS CAMPAIGNED TO HIGHLIGHT THE DANGERS OF OVER-TANNING IN THE MEDIA.** She even made a documentary about it entitled *The Truth About Tanning*.

THE ORIGINAL MUST-HAVE LOOK

The aim of the Dainty Doll range is to give pale-skinned girls an opportunity to enhance the lightness of their skin, rather than seek to darken it, which seems to be the trend today.

But contrary to this, most make-up throughout history has been designed to enhance paleness or even fake it. These ranges had significantly less benefit for the wearer, with **SOME EVEN PROVING TO BE LETHAL.**

The ancient Greeks and Romans used mercury and arsenic to achieve a pale complexion as a sign of wealth, and in the Italian Renaissance this fashion continued, with women coating their faces with arsenic and lead: **A KILLER COMBINATION, LITERALLY.**

In the sixteenth century the use of make-up was confined to the very wealthy. Queen Elizabeth I used pastes of lead, chalk and flour as a means of emphasizing the paleness that was a key part of her image of purity and virginity. Ironically **THE PRODUCTS SHE USED TO PORTRAY HER ETERNAL YOUTH ACTUALLY HASTENED HER DEATH,** having gradually poisoned her for years.

Make-up re-emerged in mainstream use in the eighteenth century, this time by both sexes, when the Georgians made extensive use of lead powder once again. Back then, **PALE SKIN WAS A MARK OF GENTILITY:** those without a tan were clearly rich enough to not need to work outdoors with the 'vulgar' working classes. In the early twentieth century paleness was seen as the epitome of chic, until tanning became fashionable in the latter half of the century.

However, since past fashions frequently provide inspiration for forward-looking designers and fashion pioneers, perhaps **NICOLA MAY SOON BE AT THE FOREFRONT OF A PALE-SKIN RENAISSANCE.**

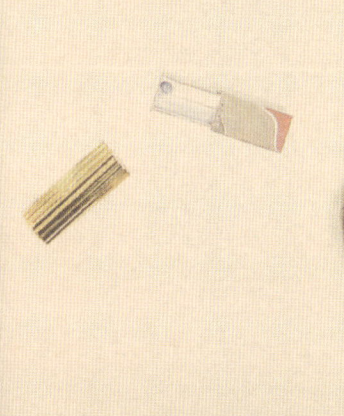

PRINCE
THE PURPLEAXXE

PURPLE-LOVING POP STAR PRINCE IS ONE OF THE MOST SUCCESSFUL MUSICIANS OF THE LAST 20 YEARS. HE HAS COLLABORATED WITH THE BIGGEST NAMES IN THE MUSIC INDUSTRY, FROM MADONNA TO BEYONCÉ AND HIS LIVE PERFORMANCES ATTRACT SOME OF THE LARGEST AUDIENCES IN THE WORLD.

When once dissatisfied with an aspect of his live act, he drew upon musical experiences from his childhood to invent a zany instrument called **THE PURPLEAXXE™**.

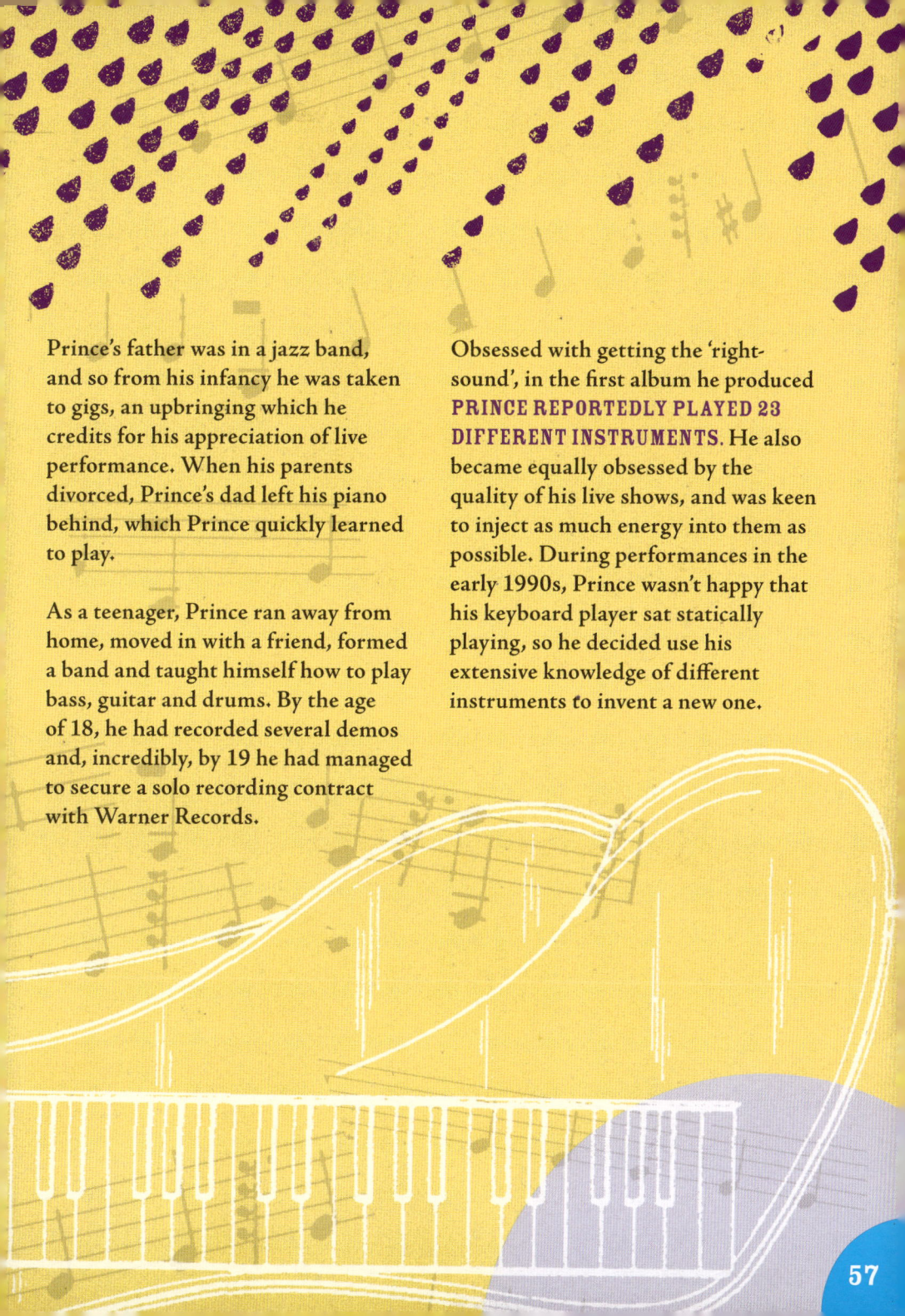

Prince's father was in a jazz band, and so from his infancy he was taken to gigs, an upbringing which he credits for his appreciation of live performance. When his parents divorced, Prince's dad left his piano behind, which Prince quickly learned to play.

As a teenager, Prince ran away from home, moved in with a friend, formed a band and taught himself how to play bass, guitar and drums. By the age of 18, he had recorded several demos and, incredibly, by 19 he had managed to secure a solo recording contract with Warner Records.

Obsessed with getting the 'right-sound', in the first album he produced **PRINCE REPORTEDLY PLAYED 23 DIFFERENT INSTRUMENTS.** He also became equally obsessed by the quality of his live shows, and was keen to inject as much energy into them as possible. During performances in the early 1990s, Prince wasn't happy that his keyboard player sat statically playing, so he decided use his extensive knowledge of different instruments to invent a new one.

In 1992, he patented THE PURPLEAXXE, a portable electronic musical keyboard which is ESSENTIALLY A TRANSLATION OF THE ELECTRIC GUITAR. It is designed to be hung around the neck of the musician and played in the same way as a guitar, enabling the performer to stride around the stage and interact with the audience.

The unique design also incorporates a double arrow that bears a striking resemblance to the symbol to which Prince later changed his name (he's since changed it back to Prince). Unfortunately, the patent is almost exclusively concerned with how the instrument looks, so details about the construction of the instrument and the keyboard structure are minimal.

PURPLEAXXE PERFORMANCES

Despite being known as a multi-instrumentalist and having invented the Purpleaxxe, PRINCE HAS NEVER ACTUALLY BEEN SEEN USING IT. Reportedly fiendishly difficult to play, only one has ever been made, and it is Prince's bandmate Tommy Barberella who actually uses it live.

In a recent interview PRINCE HAS SAID HE HAS NO PLANS TO COMMERCIALIZE HIS PURPLEAXXE so, for now, it will remain one of a kind.

STRANGE BUT TRUE...

Prince is not the only famous musician to have invented his own instrument. French electronic artist Jean Michel Jarre developed the **LASER HARP** (pictured), a bizarre and ingenious instrument that uses a set of laser lights instead of strings. Rather than plucking strings, on a Laser Harp the performer breaks the beams with their hand. The lasers are linked to a synthesizer that can detect which beam has been broken and plays the appropriate note.

Rather more tongue-in-cheek, Rolf Harris famously invented the **WOBBLEBOARD**, which is essentially a large sheet of thin wood flexed to make a whooping noise, as well as promoting the **STYLOPHONE**, a miniature synthesizer played with a metal pen – all the range in the 1960s.

Finally, who could forget **SPINAL TAP**? They blessed us with the Amp that goes up to 11.

FRANCIS FORD COPPOLA

BACK SCRATCHER'S T-SHIRT

AS A PRODUCER, DIRECTOR AND SCREENWRITER, FRANCIS FORD COPPOLA HAS WON MORE OSCARS THAN YOU CAN SHAKE A STICK AT. WIDELY ACCLAIMED AS ONE OF THE MOST INFLUENTIAL FILMMAKERS OF ALL TIME, HIS ICONIC FILMS INCLUDE *THE GODFATHER* TRILOGY, *THE RAINMAKER* AND *APOCALYPSE NOW*.

However, Francis may just have eclipsed these acclaimed cinematic masterpieces as the proud inventor of the **BACK SCRATCHER'S T-SHIRT.** You may not have heard of it, but once you know its purpose, scratching that itch will never be the same again…

Born in 1939, Francis contracted polio at age 10 and was fated to stay bedridden for long periods of time. It was during the unspeakable boredom of these hours that Francis began to use his imagination to amuse himself, developing an interest in puppetry and theatre which sowed the seeds of his prodigious filmmaking career. These polio-imposed periods of boredom and restriction also sparked the tongue-in-cheek idea Francis was later to patent.

He called it **'A GARMENT FOR IDENTIFYING A LOCATION ON THE BODY OF THE GARMENT WEARER'**, and it is, in its most basic form, a T-shirt design that incorporates a grid. The grid has reference points around it so that the wearer can accurately indicate any point on his back.

The grid design isn't exactly ideal in terms of fashion, but Francis had thought of that. The design he patented was in the form of a turtle, which carried the numbered grid on its shell. A card with the same grid comes with the T-shirt, so that the wearer can work it out without memorizing the grid.

A SCRATCHY SUCCESS?

Francis's 2006 patent argues persuasively that his invention will make the world a better, less-itchy place and will improve your daily life. He writes:

> Scratching an itch is a very common task in everyday life. It can be especially difficult, however, for a person to scratch his or her own itch when the location of the itch is in a hard-to-reach spot such as the back. Presently, a person with an itch in a hard-to-reach location must ask a second party to scratch the itch. This, in turn, requires orienting the second-party-scratcher by using a series of directions, which are often being misunderstood by the second party. For example, these instructions might include Could you scratch lower? To the left…No, the other left. Now, down lower. To the right. No, no…Too far! Back to the left. Thus, there is a need for an object that assists a person in precisely identifying a location on the person's own body for a second party.

Despite Francis's compelling argument for its usefulness, he hasn't yet launched his back-scratching T-shirt for the public to enjoy.

ANOTHER DIRECTION

Francis need not be too downhearted that his back-scratching invention hasn't yet reached the masses, as he has created a wealth of other products that have made it out into the public domain. Using the profits from *The Godfather*, Francis bought his own vineyard, called the Rubicon Estate Winery, and successfully makes and sells his own wine. He has also recently devised his own speciality food range.

His lifestyle brand, called 'Francis Ford Coppola Presents…', markets the goods from all the companies he owns, so it may not be too long before he presents to the world the Back Scratcher's T-Shirt as part of his growing product range.

EDDIE VAN HALEN

GUITAR-SOLO SUPPORT

FOUNDING MEMBER AND GUITARIST OF ROCK BAND VAN HALEN, EDDIE VAN HALEN IS PERHAPS BEST KNOWN FOR HIS 1980s HIT 'JUMP' AND FOR PLAYING THE GUITAR SOLO ON MICHAEL JACKSON'S 'BEAT IT'.

As a professional guitarist with a rock 'n' roll attitude, Eddie has always been keen to push musical boundaries by exploring different sounds and playing techniques. In 1987 he filed a patent for a **'MUSICAL INSTRUMENT SUPPORT'** that he hoped might revolutionize guitar playing. Sadly, it didn't.

During live shows, Eddie became famous for his guitar solos, and particularly for a technique called 'finger tapping'. **IT SEEMS EDDIE FOUND PLAYING SOLOS EASIER WHILE SITTING DOWN,** as he could lay his guitar facing upwards on his knees and play it with both hands. The downside of this is that it isn't a particularly rock 'n' roll image.

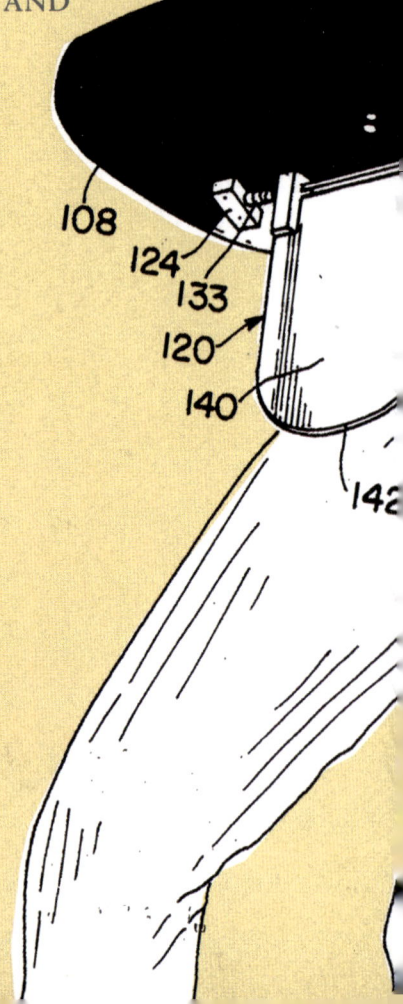

64

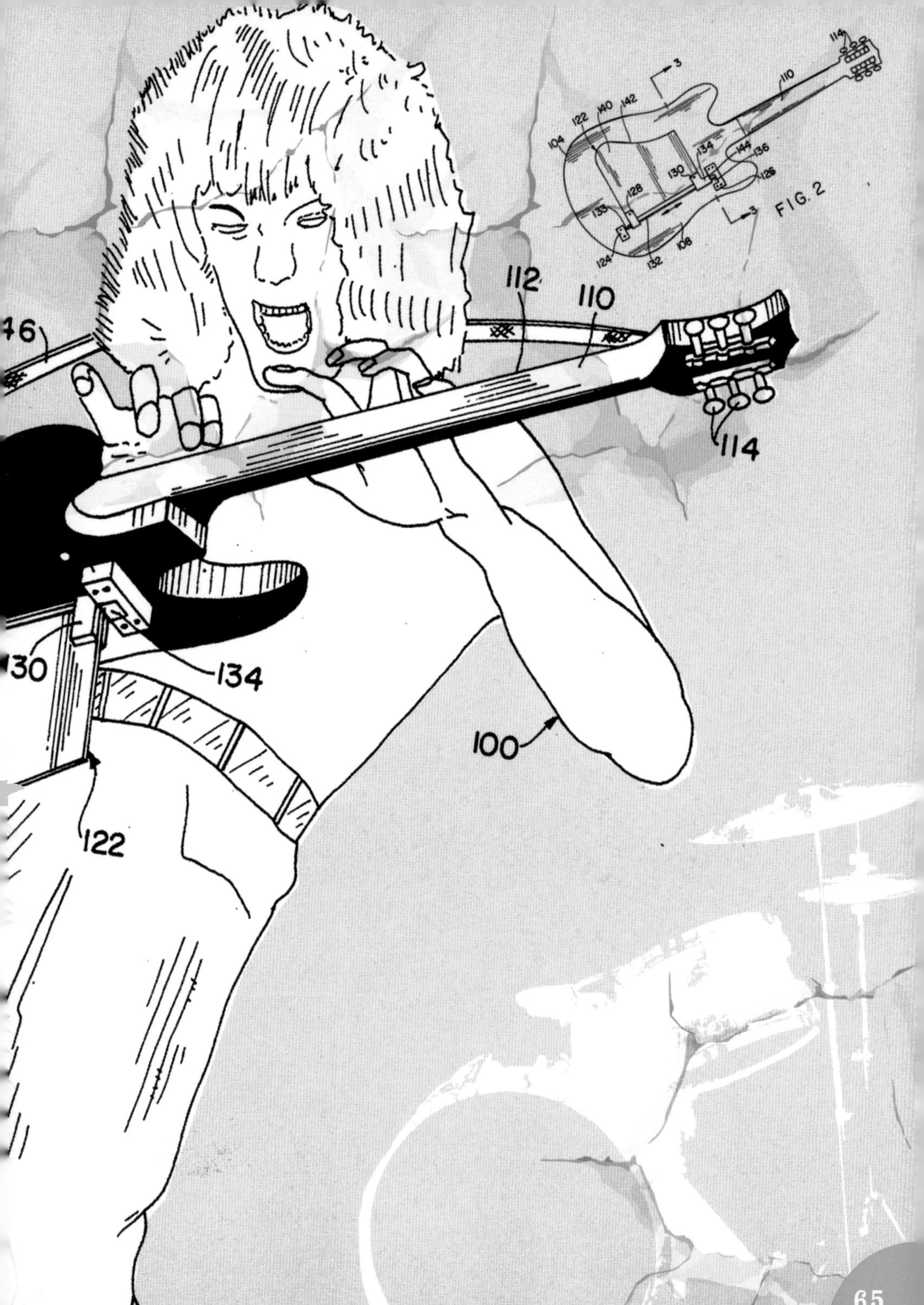

FIG. 2

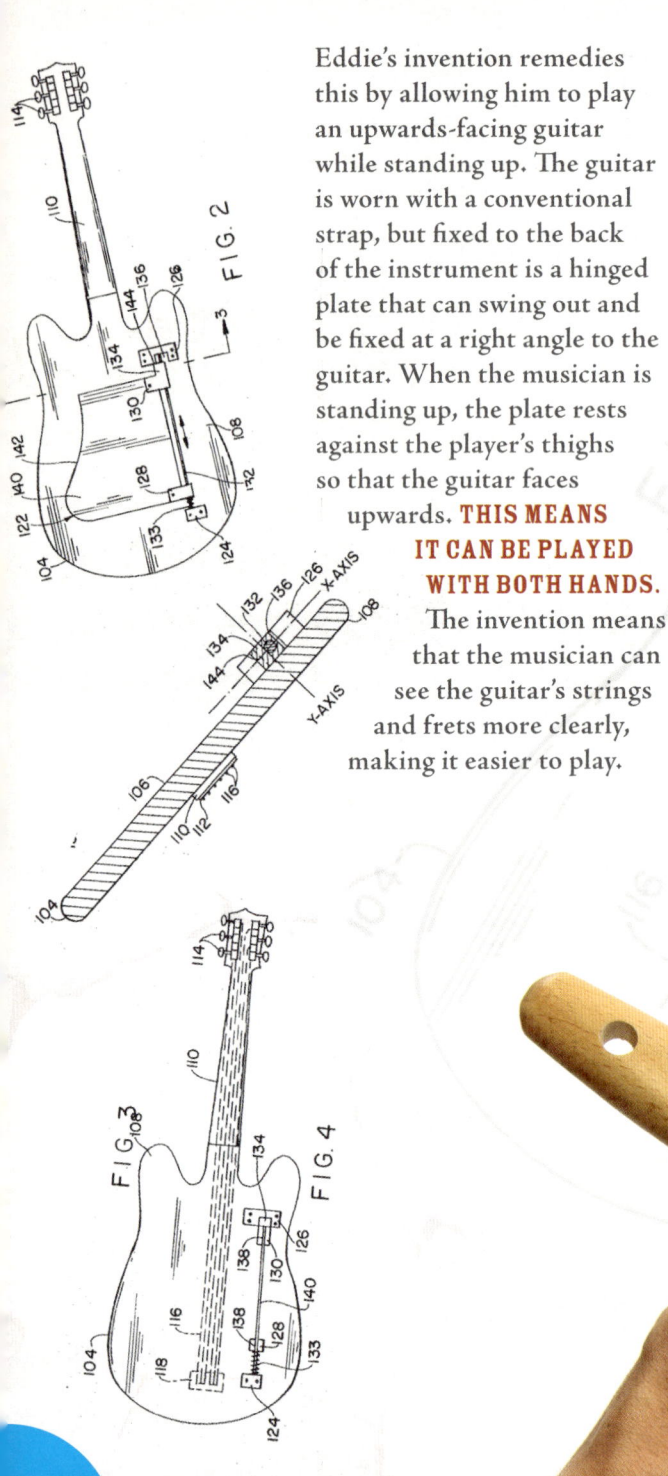

Eddie's invention remedies this by allowing him to play an upwards-facing guitar while standing up. The guitar is worn with a conventional strap, but fixed to the back of the instrument is a hinged plate that can swing out and be fixed at a right angle to the guitar. When the musician is standing up, the plate rests against the player's thighs so that the guitar faces upwards. **THIS MEANS IT CAN BE PLAYED WITH BOTH HANDS.**

The invention means that the musician can see the guitar's strings and frets more clearly, making it easier to play.

GOING SOLO: WHAT EDDIE DID NEXT

So far Eddie's solo support has not been taken up by other rock guitarists, and as a consequence he remains the only one to use it on stage. But Eddie's no quitter, and he wasn't about to give up on guitar-based inventions…

First Eddie created the 'Frankenstrat' guitar. Half Fender Stratocaster, half Gibson Les Paul, this new guitar combines a Stratocaster body with a Gibson pickup. **HE EVEN PAINTED IT HIMSELF.**

In 1995 Eddie patented the alternative design for the 'peghead' of a guitar. His invention set out how the tuning pegs for tightening

66

the guitar string could be laid out in an alternative configuration. It's more of an aesthetic development than an improvement in the function of the guitar, but, unfortunately, like the guitar-solo support, this invention didn't take off either.

Undeterred, in 2003 Eddie invented the D-Tuna, a device that lets a guitar player instantly drop the tuning of their guitar from the E to D and back again. (Eddie has been using early versions of the invention on his own guitars since the early 1990s.) In 2004 he started a company selling the D-Tuna and has finally struck inventive gold; **THE DEVICE NOW SELLS TO MUSICIANS ACROSS THE WORLD.**

GEORGE LUCAS

STAR WARS FIGURES

AMERICAN FILM PRODUCER, SCREENWRITER AND DIRECTOR GEORGE LUCAS IS BEST KNOWN FOR BEING THE CREATOR OF THE *STAR WARS* FILMS – BUT HE ALSO INVENTED MUCH MORE THAN THE FILMS' STORYLINE.

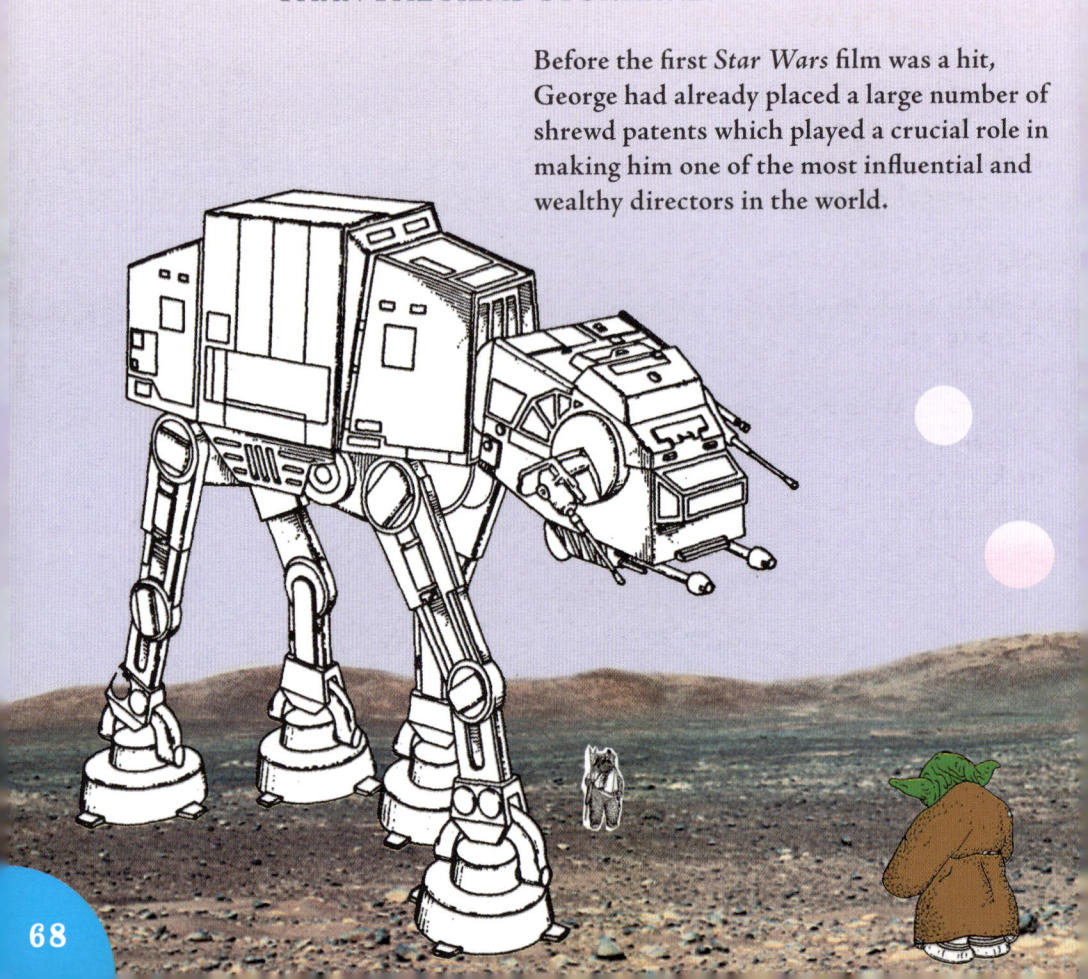

Before the first *Star Wars* film was a hit, George had already placed a large number of shrewd patents which played a crucial role in making him one of the most influential and wealthy directors in the world.

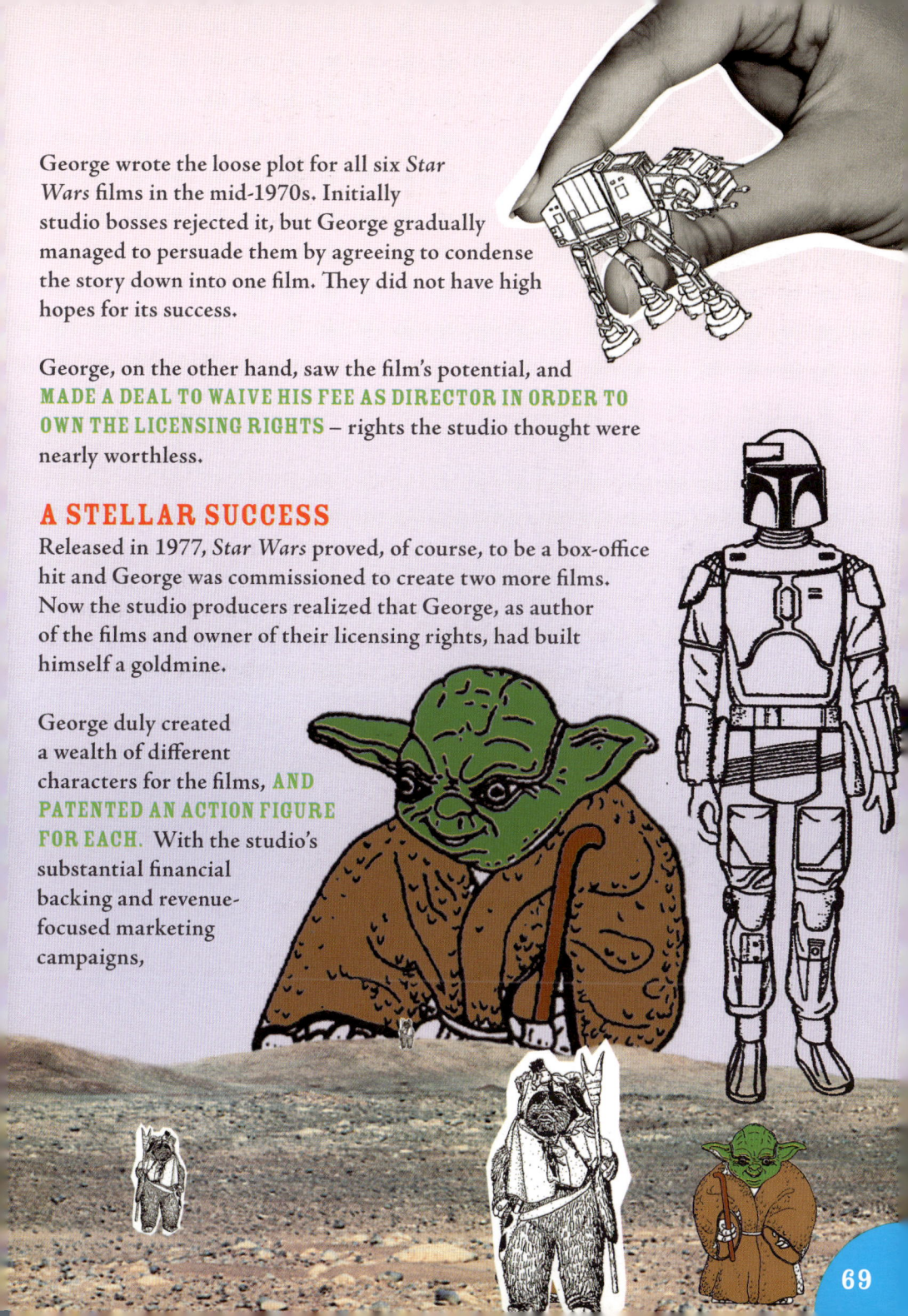

George wrote the loose plot for all six *Star Wars* films in the mid-1970s. Initially studio bosses rejected it, but George gradually managed to persuade them by agreeing to condense the story down into one film. They did not have high hopes for its success.

George, on the other hand, saw the film's potential, and **MADE A DEAL TO WAIVE HIS FEE AS DIRECTOR IN ORDER TO OWN THE LICENSING RIGHTS** – rights the studio thought were nearly worthless.

A STELLAR SUCCESS

Released in 1977, *Star Wars* proved, of course, to be a box-office hit and George was commissioned to create two more films. Now the studio producers realized that George, as author of the films and owner of their licensing rights, had built himself a goldmine.

George duly created a wealth of different characters for the films, **AND PATENTED AN ACTION FIGURE FOR EACH.** With the studio's substantial financial backing and revenue-focused marketing campaigns,

George had all his promotional work done for him. Each new character, machine, robot, spaceship or creature became a registered idea in George's name. **HE MAY AS WELL HAVE HAD A LICENCE TO PRINT MONEY**, earning over $2 billion from the *Star Wars* franchise.

IN A GALAXY FAR, FAR AWAY...OR MAYBE NOT...

George Lucas invented lots of space-age gadgets and gizmos to make the *Star Wars* films come alive, but would any of them be feasible here on Earth?

1. ROBOTIC HAND: Fitted to Luke Skywalker at the end of *The Empire Strikes Back*. A fully functional replacement for the human hand, complete with thought control, may be closer than you think. In 2009, an Italian amputee became the first person in the world to be given a robotic hand that can be controlled by thoughts. Surgeons implanted electrodes in his arm where connections had been severed and his robotic hand obeys the commands it receives from his brain in 95% of instances.

2. HOVER-CARS: Used thoughout the *Star Wars* films. Hover-cars are now commercially available. The Moller M200G Hover-Car can hover at 10 feet and reach speeds of up to 50 mph. It looks like a small flying saucer and it sells for between £90k and £125k. Best of all, you don't need a licence to drive one!

3. LIGHTSABERS: These plasma swords are the weapon of choice for any discerning Jedi Knight. In theory this invention is possible. Plasma is essentially a gas containing charged particles, which means it could be formed into a sword shape using a magnetic field. It is also possible to cut and weld metal using plasma. However, the main limitation is the amount of energy required. If you did manage to construct a working lightsaber, all battles would have to take place in the vicinity of a huge generator or a plug socket, which could be a bit of a drag.

D'YOU KNOW WHAT THEY SHOULD MAKE...?
Here are some other potential inventions, inspired by *Star Wars*:

3D Projectors: Creating life-like 3D projections in your living room would revolutionize television and computer games.

Walking Vehicles: Walking vehicles would be great on rough terrain since there'd be no danger of getting a puncture and obstacles could simply be stepped over.

R2D2: Friendly dustbin-like robots that can coerce any computer into doing exactly what you want, fix electrical devices, open any security door, and help you drive your car, would make daily life a doddle.

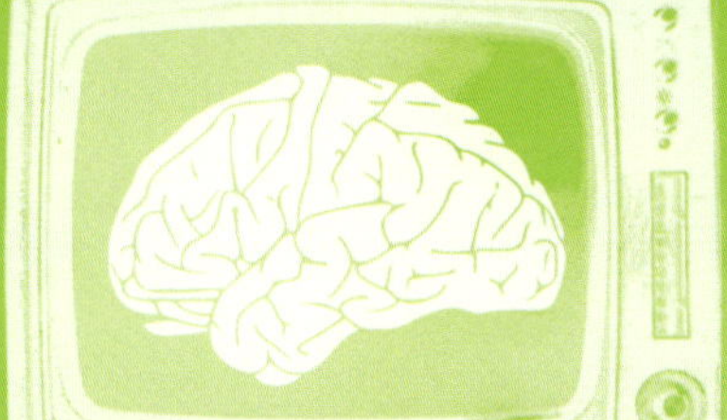

3. TV PERSONALITIES

JON SNOW

ANTI-THEFT GRAVITY-INTENSIFYING BICYCLE

AS A JOURNALIST AND PRESENTER OF *CHANNEL 4 NEWS*, JON SNOW IS CONSTANTLY AT THE FOREFRONT OF NEW DEVELOPMENTS IN TECHNOLOGY AS WELL AS IN POLITICS. COMBINING A LOVE OF TECHNOLOGY WITH HIS LOVE OF HIS PREFERRED MODE OF TRANSPORT, THE BICYCLE (HE IS PRESIDENT OF THE BRITISH CYCLISTS' TOURING CLUB), JON CAME UP WITH A GROUNDBREAKING IDEA FOR AN INVENTION.

❛ I'm a keen cyclist and usually get around London on my bike. However, over the last six months I have had two bikes stolen, which has put a bit of a dampener on things. It's quite frustrating.

Although, thieves permitting, I have my own bike, I tried the new Boris bikes when I was writing an article about the cycle-hire scheme. What struck me the most about the bikes was how heavy they were.

They are really quite chunky, and hard to carry, too, but it was this inconvenience that gave me an idea for a futuristic science-fiction-inspired anti-theft bike.

My invention is a bike that is fitted with a gravity-intensifier, which would mean that at the touch of a button it would be too heavy for a thief to move, making it unstealable!

The anti-theft device simply turns up the gravity of the bike.

Nothing else about it would change – except for the fact that it became anchored to the ground. It'd be a delight not to have to worry about having it stolen, particularly when I need to zip across town to present breaking news! '

Jon chooses to cycle around London, not just because cycling helps him to keep fit, but because as a journalist a bike enables him to stay connected with the city and (quite literally) with the 'man on the street'.

Creating the unstealable bike clearly underlines the value he puts on the humble bicycle, but could this idea ever work? Although altering gravity sounds like fantasy, one group of physicists find the idea so tantalizing that they think they can make it a reality.

DID SOMEONE TURN THE GRAVITY UP?

In the 1950s, a branch of physics emerged that was concerned with gravity control. One theory put forward by these physicists suggests that gravity can be manipulated using a **'GRAVITY CONTROL CELL'**. The theory goes that an object (such as Jon's bike) placed close to the cell would exhibit a weight decrease. It may be possible to 'turn up' the gravity and make objects heavier.

Furthermore, the theory states that it may be possible to convert gravitational energy into rotational mechanical energy by means of a 'gravitational motor'. This is, in essence, an engine that manipulates gravity to create propulsion. Inspired by this idea, a US businessman named Roger Babson established the Gravity Research Foundation to investigate such technologies as a possible means of space travel. Though it conducted almost two decades of research, the foundation closed in the late 1960s, leaving gravity motors to exist only in the realms of science fiction.

Pros and cons of 'Zero Gravity'

Pros:
+ No more diets! You instantly weigh less
+ You can spend all day lying on your back, floating around in the air
+ Reaching objects on the top shelf is no longer an issue

Cons:
− Sleeping is made difficult by all the objects you bump into
− Going to the toilet is messy
− You could fly off into the atmosphere, never to return.

JOHNNY BALL

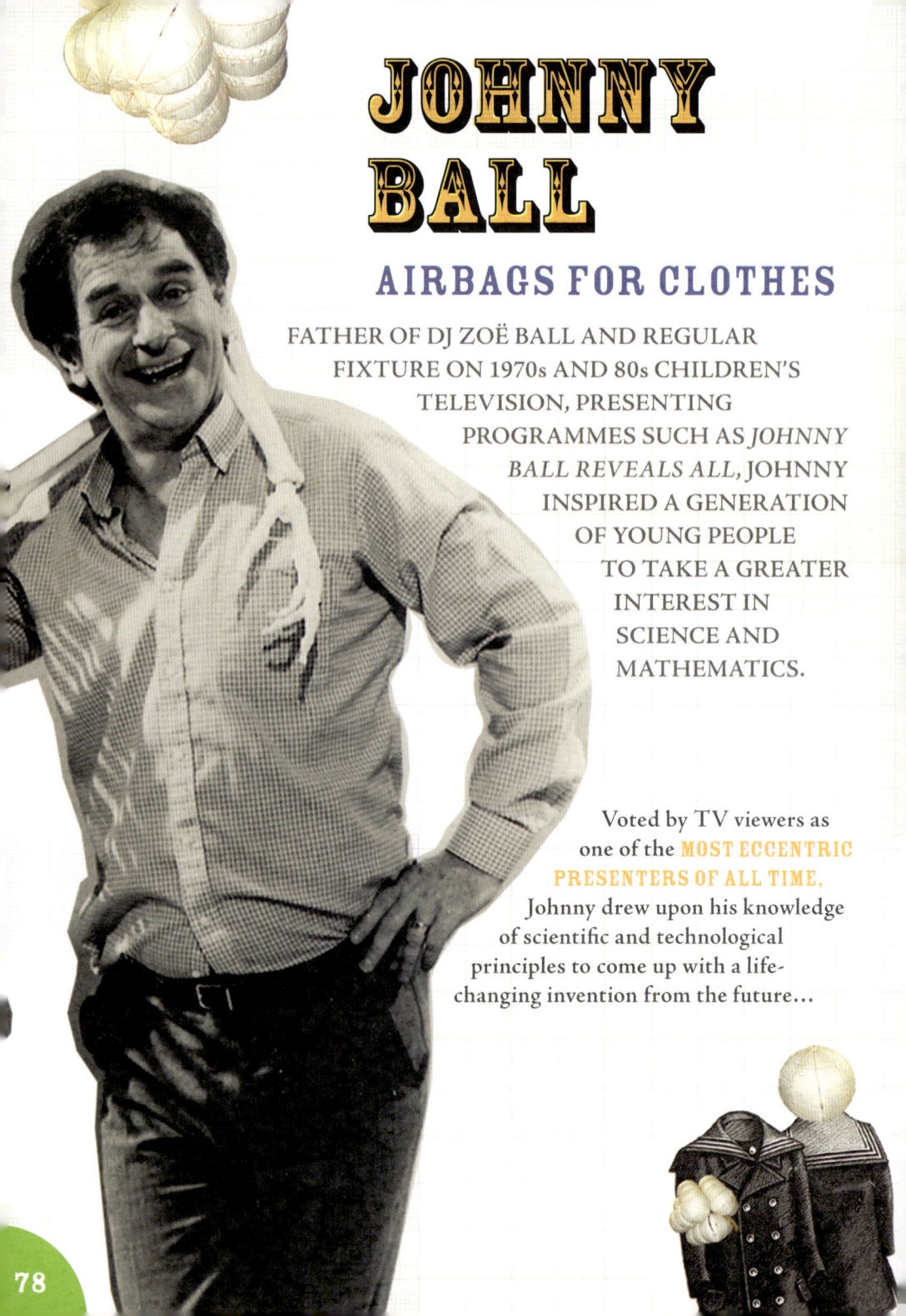

AIRBAGS FOR CLOTHES

FATHER OF DJ ZOË BALL AND REGULAR FIXTURE ON 1970s AND 80s CHILDREN'S TELEVISION, PRESENTING PROGRAMMES SUCH AS *JOHNNY BALL REVEALS ALL*, JOHNNY INSPIRED A GENERATION OF YOUNG PEOPLE TO TAKE A GREATER INTEREST IN SCIENCE AND MATHEMATICS.

Voted by TV viewers as one of the **MOST ECCENTRIC PRESENTERS OF ALL TIME**, Johnny drew upon his knowledge of scientific and technological principles to come up with a life-changing invention from the future…

'My invention is to have airbags sewn into our clothes, and anything where falling over is a hazard. When we take the tumble, the bags will inflate and we will roll – rather than crash – to the floor.

They use exactly the same technology as car airbags, deploying a soft balloon just in time to save you from injury. They are automatically activated when you fall, or when sensors detect an imminent collision.

If everyone had one, they would certainly change the world in strange and bizarre ways…

The airbags would be ideal for the contestants on *Dancing on Ice* who can't seem to stop falling over, so sequin-covered versions should be issued to all skaters. Helium-filled versions of the airbags would be a tremendous innovation for racing jockeys. If they fell off over a jump, they could be tethered to their horse so that they float safely in the air while the horse tows them on to the finish line.

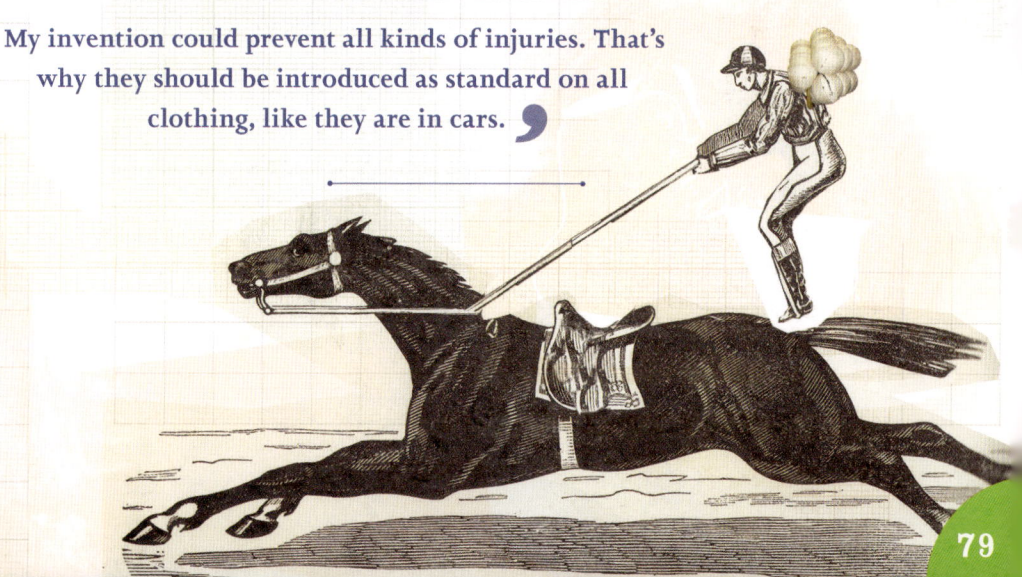

My invention could prevent all kinds of injuries. That's why they should be introduced as standard on all clothing, like they are in cars.'

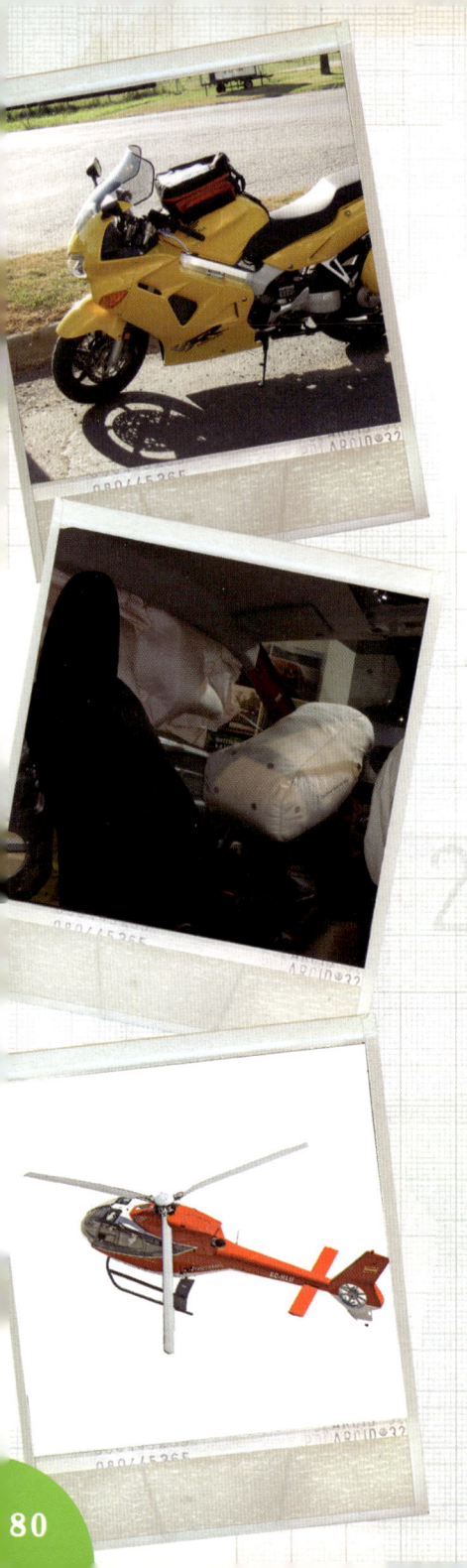

As a grandfather and advocate of science and engineering, it follows that **JOHNNY WOULD LIKE TO DEVELOP A TECHNICAL SOLUTION TO KEEP PEOPLE SAFE**. This slightly eccentric idea is likely to have been drawn from the technical knowledge that Johnny gained by working at the De Havilland Aircraft Company and the three years he spent in the RAF. So, could it be made?

AIRBAGS IN CLOTHES - IS IT JUST HOT AIR?

Airbags were first patented in 1952, though it was not until 20 years afterwards that the idea was first commercialized and taken up by the motor industry. Since their initial use in cars, airbags have found applications in boats, aircraft and helicopters. However, the technology to make Johnny's vision come true is most likely to come from developments in motorcycle racing.

Since it is a notoriously dangerous sport, motorcycle racers wear leather suits to protect themselves in the event that they fall off the bike at speed and slide along the road. An Italian company have recently taken the protection offered by motorcycle leathers one step further and **HAVE INCORPORATED AIRBAGS TO CREATE AN 'AIRBAG SUIT'**. The suit, which is now being used by a handful of top Moto GP motorcycle racers, uses sophisticated gyroscopic and impact sensors to detect when the rider is about to fall from their bike. When triggered, the whole suit inflates and special back, shoulder and head braces are deployed to ensure that the spine and neck are protected.

After a decade of development, the company says it's close to bringing an airbag suit to the market, so Johnny may soon see his vision become a reality. Music to the ears of Johnny Knoxville and daredevils everywhere!

Do's and Dont's for Using Airbag Clothing

Do:

- use if you are performing dangerous stunts
- use if you have a dangerous job
- use if you are accident prone, or have a bad feeling about the day ahead

Don't:

- use in confined spaces (such as on the Tube or train, as tempting as it may be to distance yourself from other passengers)
- set them off on purpose just to make people jump

KIRSTEN O'BRIEN

FOLDABLE SKIS

COMEDIENNE AND TV PRESENTER OF BBC3 DOCUMENTARIES AND MORNING TV, KIRSTEN O'BRIEN HAS TAUGHT A GENERATION OF KIDS TO DRAW. AS THE HOST OF KIDS TV SHOW *SMART*, SHE HAS ENCOURAGED COUNTLESS YOUNGSTERS TO BE ARTISTIC AND CREATIVE.

Her expertise with a pot of glue and some felt-tip pens is the envy of any *Blue Peter* presenter, but **KIRSTEN MIGHT ALSO HAVE THE SKILLS NEEDED TO MAKE IT AS AN INVENTOR.** On a winter holiday, Kirsten realized it was possible to solve a long-standing problem faced by fellow skiers…

> Going skiing is always fun – the snow, the slopes, the après-ski – the only thing that isn't fun is lugging all the kit around. I get pretty annoyed when I've paid a fortune to hire my gear and have to lug it all around about whenever I'm off the slopes.

This is especially annoying at the end of a long day, when I have to find my way back from a snow slope to wherever I'm staying. Trying to juggle a map, skis, poles and anything else I might be carrying is tricky at the best of times, let alone after a day's worth of skiing. That's when I find skis really cumbersome. I'm always dropping them and ending up in a mess.

But I think I have the solution – foldable skis! My Foldable Ski enables skiers to carry their kit much more easily – that would be life-changing, really. The clever design means that they could fold up quickly and easily so that you could put them in a shoulder bag or rucksack in an instant.

The Foldable Ski means that more people could own their own gear, because it would be much less hassle to pack and travel with. This helps the ski manufacturers no end! Not to mention how much it benefits the general public too – getting a ski in the face on a ski lift would finally be a thing of the past.

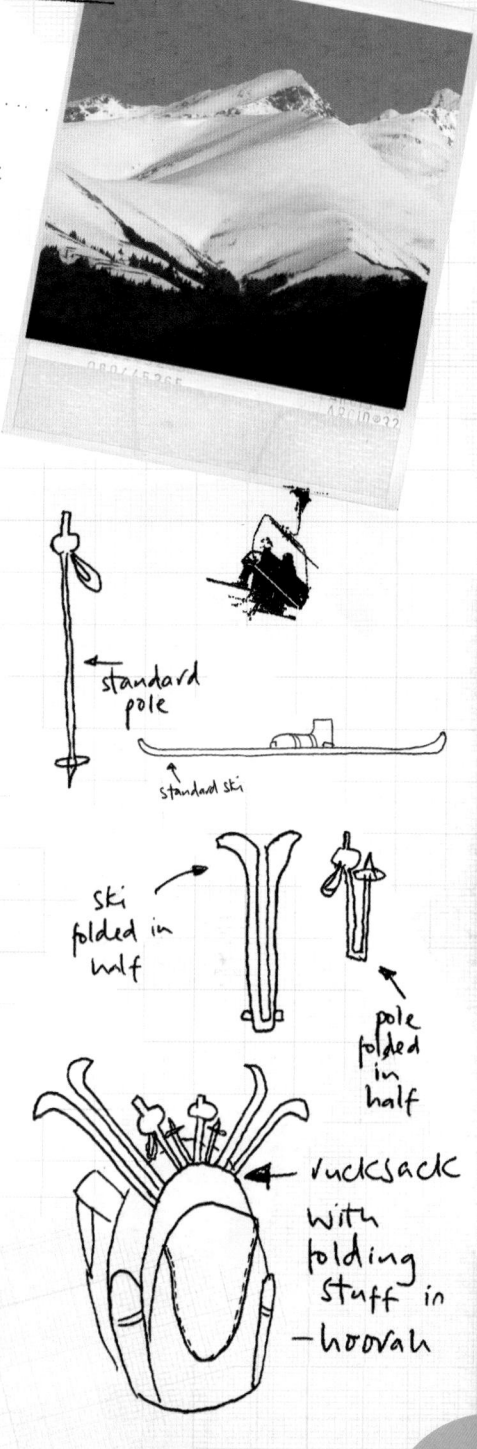

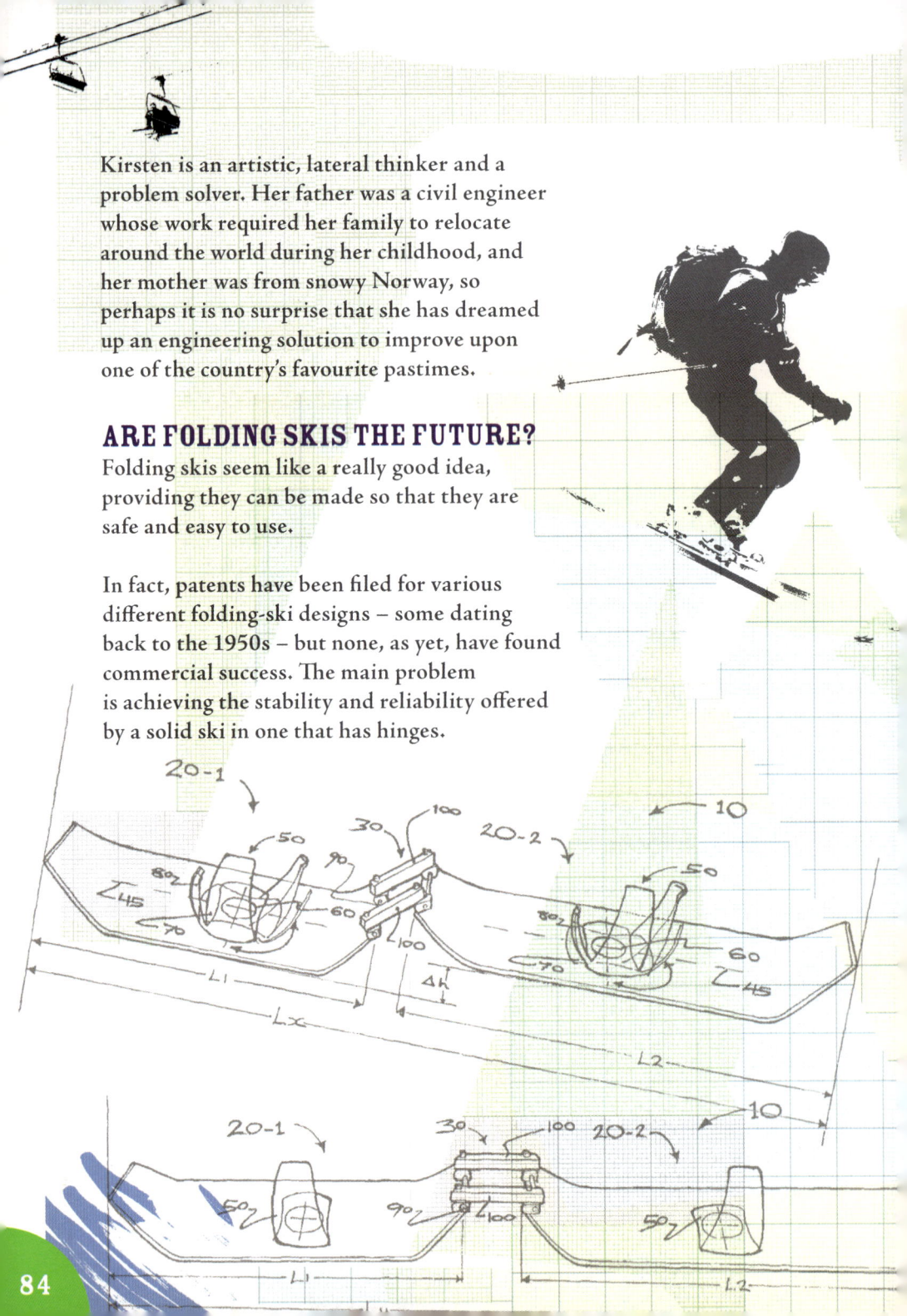

Kirsten is an artistic, lateral thinker and a problem solver. Her father was a civil engineer whose work required her family to relocate around the world during her childhood, and her mother was from snowy Norway, so perhaps it is no surprise that she has dreamed up an engineering solution to improve upon one of the country's favourite pastimes.

ARE FOLDING SKIS THE FUTURE?

Folding skis seem like a really good idea, providing they can be made so that they are safe and **easy to use**.

In fact, **patents have** been filed for various different **folding-ski** designs – some dating back to **the 1950s** – but none, as yet, have found commercial success. The main problem is achieving the stability and reliability offered by a solid **ski** in one that has hinges.

But, believe it or not, scientists are in the process of developing a potential solution: **SELF-HEALING MATERIALS.**

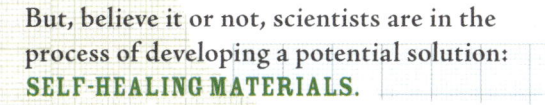

The idea is that, in the future, **A MATERIAL WILL BE ENGINEERED TO HEAL ITSELF, LIKE THE HUMAN BODY.** In the same way that the pieces of a broken bone fuse together without any help, **IT MIGHT BE POSSIBLE TO CREATE OTHER THINGS THAT CAN MEND AUTONOMOUSLY.** The aim is to create something that can be folded, broken or shattered and then repair itself.

Scientists think that one means of doing this would be to develop a surface impregnated with microscopic capsules of gluey resin. When the surface breaks or cracks, the resin will leak out, fill the gaps and set hard, **MAKING THE OBJECT WHOLE AGAIN**.

So, Kirsten, watch this space. If self-healing materials are successfully created, it might just be possible to develop a ski that would be completely solid when in use, but could then be folded away at the end of the day.

SUZI PERRY

THE AIRSTREAM TELEPORTER

PRESENTER SUZI PERRY IS A MOTOR-SPORT ENTHUSIAST AND SELF-CONFESSED FAN OF ALL THINGS NEW AND ADVENTUROUS. AS A PRESENTER OF *THE GADGET SHOW*, SUZI HAS ACCESS TO ALL THE LATEST GADGETS AND TECHNOLOGY FROM AROUND THE WORLD.

She has also jetted off to different countries to present the MotoGP motorcycling championship, often visiting several different continents every year, which led her to suggest an inspired invention.

❝ I used to spend an enormous amount of my life travelling, but there were only so many airline meals and baggage carousels I could handle. I thought – If only there were a cozy, comfortable home-from-home that I could take around with me – but one that avoided the need for a HGV licence or degree in advanced towing. That's when I dreamed up my invention: the Airstream Teleporter.

The concept is simple – it's a remake of the classic staples of caravan life in a twenty-second-century way. It uses the iconic aluminium caravan from the oldest remaining caravan manufacturer, Airstream. Over 80 years after its aerodynamic design was introduced it still looks futuristic, so there's no need to change the exterior! (Well, apart from removing the tow hitch.) At the heart of the Airstream sits the teleporter itself, ready to dematerialize and relocate the whole caravan and its contents.

A typical folding table in the front of the caravan houses mind-controlled navigation hardware. If I think of home, it'll take me there. Though admittedly this runs the risk that I'll become trapped in an endless loop of shoe shops, it's a risk I'm willing to take.

87

With the Airstream Teleporter there is no check-in, no jet lag, and no deep-vein thrombosis socks. When you flick a switch in the Teleporter (first making sure all loose crockery is safely stowed and cupboard doors are fastened shut, of course), it will dematerialize, then instantly reconstruct itself atom by atom wherever I choose. It simply teleports from location to location. This would put the glamour back into travel.

TELEPORTATION – FACT OR SCIENCE FICTION?

Motivated by her itinerant lifestyle, Suzi has come up with a solution that, she hopes, will make such journeys much more civilized, but could it ever be made?

Teleportation involves dematerializing an object in one place, sending the details of that object's precise atomic structure, and reconstructing it in a new location. It sounds like science fiction but, in fact, Suzi's Airstream Transporter may actually be possible.

Remarkably, **IN 1993 PHYSICIST CHARLES BENNETT PROVED THAT QUANTUM TELEPORTATION WAS POSSIBLE** – but only if the original object being teleported was destroyed. He pointed out that this shouldn't be a problem, in theory, because an exact copy of the object will appear the very second the original is destroyed. So in 1998 the first ever teleportation was successfully performed, on a single sub-atomic particle.

For Suzi and her Airstream caravan to be transported, her teleporter would have to pinpoint and analyse all of the 1 trillion trillion atoms in her body, the structure of the caravan and its contents. That sounds like a bit of a challenge, but with computers becoming more and more powerful, this should, in theory, be possible someday.

So, like a giant three-dimensional fax machine, **SUZI'S TELEPORTER INVENTION REALLY COULD EXIST.** She'd be able to scan, send and instantaneously re-create herself in a new location surrounded by her favourite possessions, arriving as fresh as a daisy.

THE PROS AND CONS OF TELEPORTATION

Pros:

+ No queues at the airport

+ No need to carry luggage

Cons:

- There's no opportunity to unwind and enjoy the journey

- No Duty Free shopping

- The slightest computer glitch and you will arrive in your destination as mush

PETER SNOW

QUICK GRUB

PRESENTER PETER SNOW IS SOMETHING OF A BRAINBOX AND INNOVATION EXPERT, HAVING HOSTED BBC's *TOMORROW'S WORLD*, RADIO 4's QUIZ *BRAIN OF BRITAIN* AND BEEN ITN's SPACE CORRESPONDENT FOR THE LUNAR LANDINGS.

Well known for his exuberant personality in front of the camera, Peter leads an equally hectic lifestyle off-screen too. That's why he invented **QUICK GRUB**, the perfect fuel for manic days.

> I'm always having to read books and papers, and I travel a great deal for the BBC. Because I am so busy, stopping to eat is often a nuisance, and it's not an unusual occurrence that I don't have time for a decent meal.
>
> The nights that I presented the Election results were also problematic for this reason. It was all terrifically exciting, but would usually involve staying up all night to explain various political implications as the results came through.

> So I have an invention idea called Quick Grub, a healthy and nutritious meal in a capsule that you can easily take. The body can absorb it extra quickly and it keeps you going when you're in a rush, no problem.

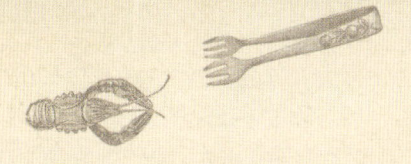

Finding time to eat properly is a recurrent problem for anyone with a busy schedule, so could Quick Grub provide the solution?

A WHOLE NEW MEANING TO FAST FOOD

The concept of Quick Grub draws on generations of sci-fi wishful thinking and fantasy, but for a limited few it is actually a reality. Since the early 1960s scientists have been working on low-weight, high-nutrition foods that can be simply ingested – just like Quick Grub. **THE RESULT WAS SPACE FOOD!**

For space travel, the goal is to minimize the weight and volume of the food carried, whilst providing enough sustenance to keep the astronauts healthy; this is because **IT TAKES ABOUT A KILOGRAM OF FUEL TO PUT ONE GRAM OF SOMETHING INTO SPACE.**

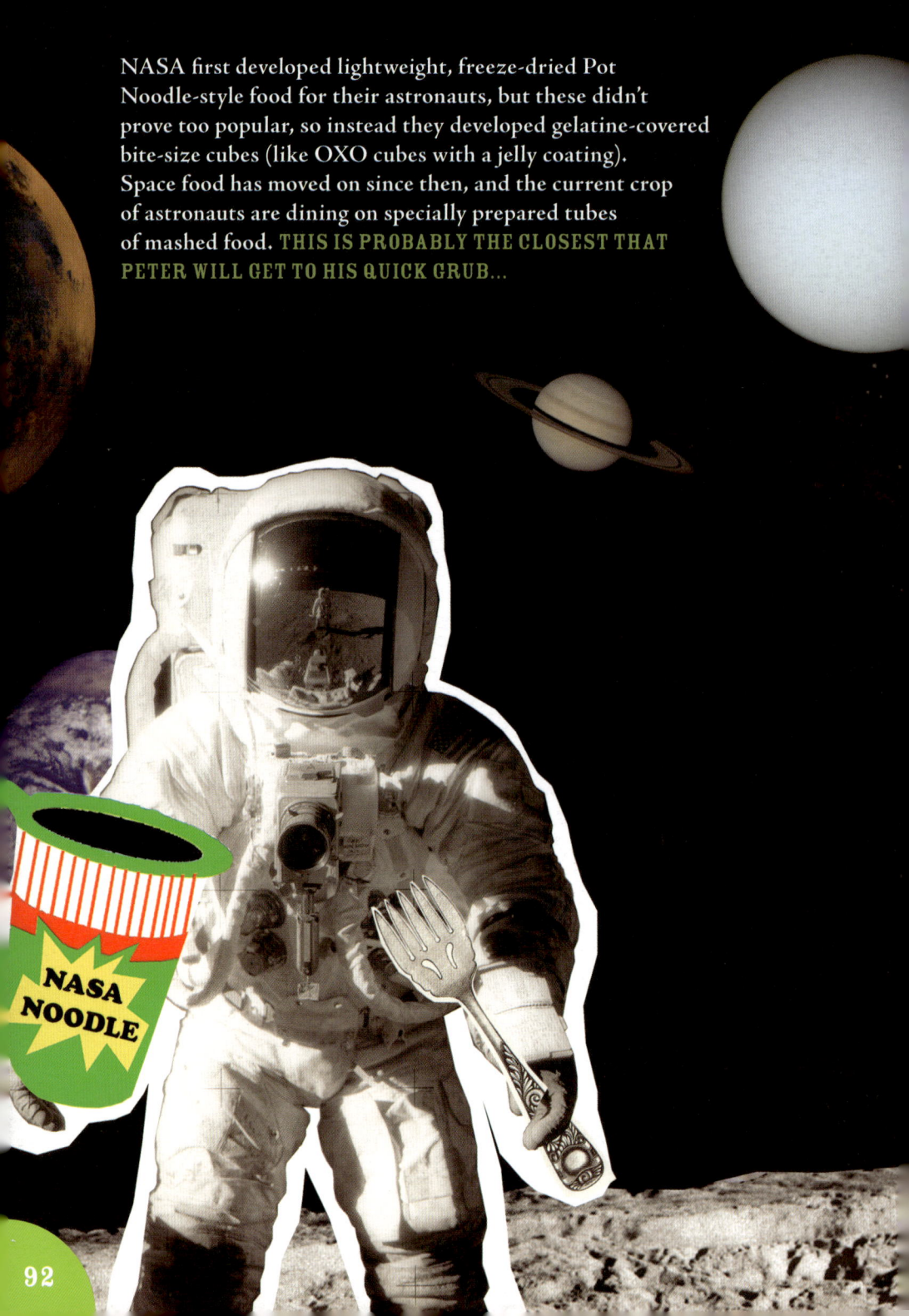

NASA first developed lightweight, freeze-dried Pot Noodle-style food for their astronauts, but these didn't prove too popular, so instead they developed gelatine-covered bite-size cubes (like OXO cubes with a jelly coating). Space food has moved on since then, and the current crop of astronauts are dining on specially prepared tubes of mashed food. **THIS IS PROBABLY THE CLOSEST THAT PETER WILL GET TO HIS QUICK GRUB...**

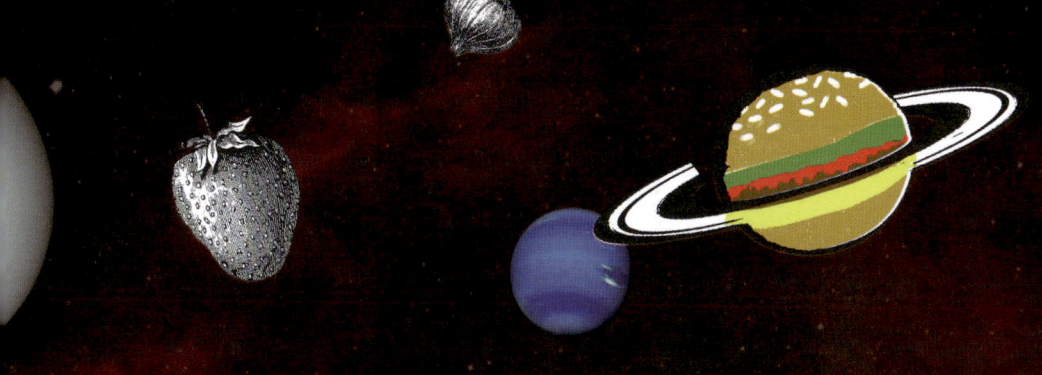

SPACE-RACE SPIN-OFFS

Whilst presenting *Tomorrow's World*, Peter Snow introduced to our screens a number of products that were derived from NASA technology. A handful of these have since found their way into mainstream medicine, ordinary homes and our everyday lives.

1. CORDLESS POWER TOOLS:
Every DIY fan's favourite toy, cordless power tools were originally developed to allow astronauts to work on the Space Shuttle whilst in orbit.

2. SMOKE DETECTORS:
Designed in the 1970s for use in Skylab, the United States' first space station, smoke detectors quickly found their way into homes around the world.

3. MEDICAL IMAGING:
(CAT and MRI scanners): Created to identify and fix imperfections in aerospace structures (like castings, rocket motors and nozzles), CAT and MRI scanners are now widely used to scan the human body for tumours and other abnormalities.

Contrary to common belief, NASA did not invent Velcro or Teflon. It's also a myth that NASA spent millions developing a pen that would still work in space, while the Russians took a pencil! All astronauts used a pencil initially, but there was always a danger that broken lead could find its way into instrument panels and cause short circuits, so a pressurized pen (useable in zero gravity) was developed independently by an inventor called Paul Fisher. In 1967, NASA bought 400 of these pens for $2.95 each.

LISA ROGERS

SWISS ARMY MAKE-UP KIT

TV PRESENTER, ACTRESS AND MODEL LISA ROGERS HAS PRESENTED MOTORING, SPORTS AND MUSIC PROGRAMMES, AND SHE HAS ALSO APPEARED IN THE CULT GANGSTER FILM *LOCK, STOCK AND TWO SMOKING BARRELS*.

However, she is perhaps best known for presenting **SCRAPHEAP CHALLENGE**, a television programme in which teams compete to construct a machine or device using only what they can scavenge from a scrap heap.

Being a resourceful and practical type herself, Lisa would like to invent a smart product to ensure women everywhere look their best, even if they find themselves in the middle of a scrap heap.

" My idea is to invent the cosmetic version of a penknife. It would be like a 'Swiss Army Make-Up Kit', a girl's secret weapon: great in emergencies and even better in daily life! I'm sure there'd be a market for it!

On the outside it has two flat metal chambers, each with a slot. One side would hold tissues, the other wet wipes: perfect for all your cleansing needs. These can be easily accessed at a moment's notice, and could also be refilled since the top of the chamber would click back to fit in refills.

The two cleaning chambers slide apart to reveal all the make-up essentials that a girl needs. A nail file, a small black refillable mascara, a tube of concealer, a wand of multi-purpose blush/eye/lip colour and a tiny tube of lip gloss.

The Swiss Army Make-Up Kit fits in your handbag without any trouble and can stay there at all times. It has everything you could possibly need in a beauty emergency. "

Lisa is a regular on British TV and radio, and something of a tomboy in areas she covers. She is a rugby presenter for BBC Sport Wales, hosts Sky One's motoring programme *Vroom Vroom* and has presented *Match of the Day*. However, she is also a regular panellist on ITV's *Loose Women* and co-hosts a radio show entitled *Girl Talk*. Lisa's brainchild cleverly addresses her need to look good without compromising her tomboy outlook. But can a cosmetic tool be created that combines practicality and elegance in this way?

CUTTING-EDGE DESIGN

Lisa could offer her invention to Wenger S.A. and Victorinox A.G., who developed the first Swiss Army knife for the Swiss Armed Forces. The Swiss Army Make-Up Kit would be an interesting development in a long line of Swiss Army knives. Since its invention in 1897, **THE KNIFE'S DESIGN HAS BECOME GRADUALLY MORE SPECIALIZED**, and now there are versions for electricians, gardeners and even golfers.

These days they come in all shapes and sizes, the biggest of which is 25cm wide and incorporates 85 different tools – not something that would fit it your pocket so easily, but surely useful in an awful lot of different situations!

In fact, Wenger S.A. and Victorinox A.G. pride themselves on updating their knives to make them as useful as possible. **THE 2010 VERSION OF THE KNIFE INCLUDES A LASER POINTER, A 32GB DETACHABLE FLASH DRIVE AND BLUETOOTH**: all modern-day tools that reflect twenty-first-century living.

The Swiss Army Make-Up Kit would make an interesting addition to their product range and, if Lisa is representative of the market, would be genuinely useful and saleable.

SCRAP-HEAP GADGETS

Not all products are as useful as those offered by the manufacturers of Swiss Army Knives. A 2010 survey estimated that almost **£1 BILLION WORTH OF GADGETS BOUGHT AS GIFTS END UP GOING STRAIGHT TO THE SCRAP HEAP.**

Around a third of us have been given a gadget that we never or hardly ever use.

Digital photo frames, foot spas and blenders top the list of unused gifts. Other gifts best avoided are lady shavers, desk-top vacuum cleaners, candy-floss machines, electric shoe polishers and shrinkwrap machines.

Top Reasons for Shunning a Gadget

- 39% did not have time to use it
- 18% couldn't understand the instructions
- 10% used the device but didn't want to keep cleaning it
- 8% didn't like the colour
- 6% didn't like the person that gave it to them

4. COOKS & SHOWMEN

JAMIE OLIVER

FLAVOUR SHAKER

CELEBRITY CHEF JAMIE OLIVER IS NOT ONLY A SUCCESSFUL RESTAURANT OWNER, CAMPAIGNER AND AUTHOR, BUT HE IS ALSO AN INVENTOR. WHILE MANY CELEBRITIES ENDORSE OR SOURCE EXISTING PRODUCTS TO BUILD UP A PRODUCT RANGE IN THEIR OWN NAME, JAMIE HAS ACTUALLY INVENTED A BESTSELLING PRODUCT HIMSELF – THE FLAVOUR SHAKER.

> I was in my kitchen a few years ago bashing up some ingredients in my pestle and mortar and I suddenly thought to myself that there must be an easier and quicker way of bashing and grinding your herbs and spices together...Some way that isn't messy and doesn't take as much time.
>
> I've never come across anything in the shops that has come close to a good pestle and mortar, though. I put the thought to the back of my mind, but it kept reappearing every time I was making a dressing or a marinade. I was sure there was a way of coming up with some sort of gadget that you could put all your ingredients into and just shake them all together. The short of things that'd be great to "smoosh-up" soft fruit to make a smoothie, or crush up ingredients to release their flavours.

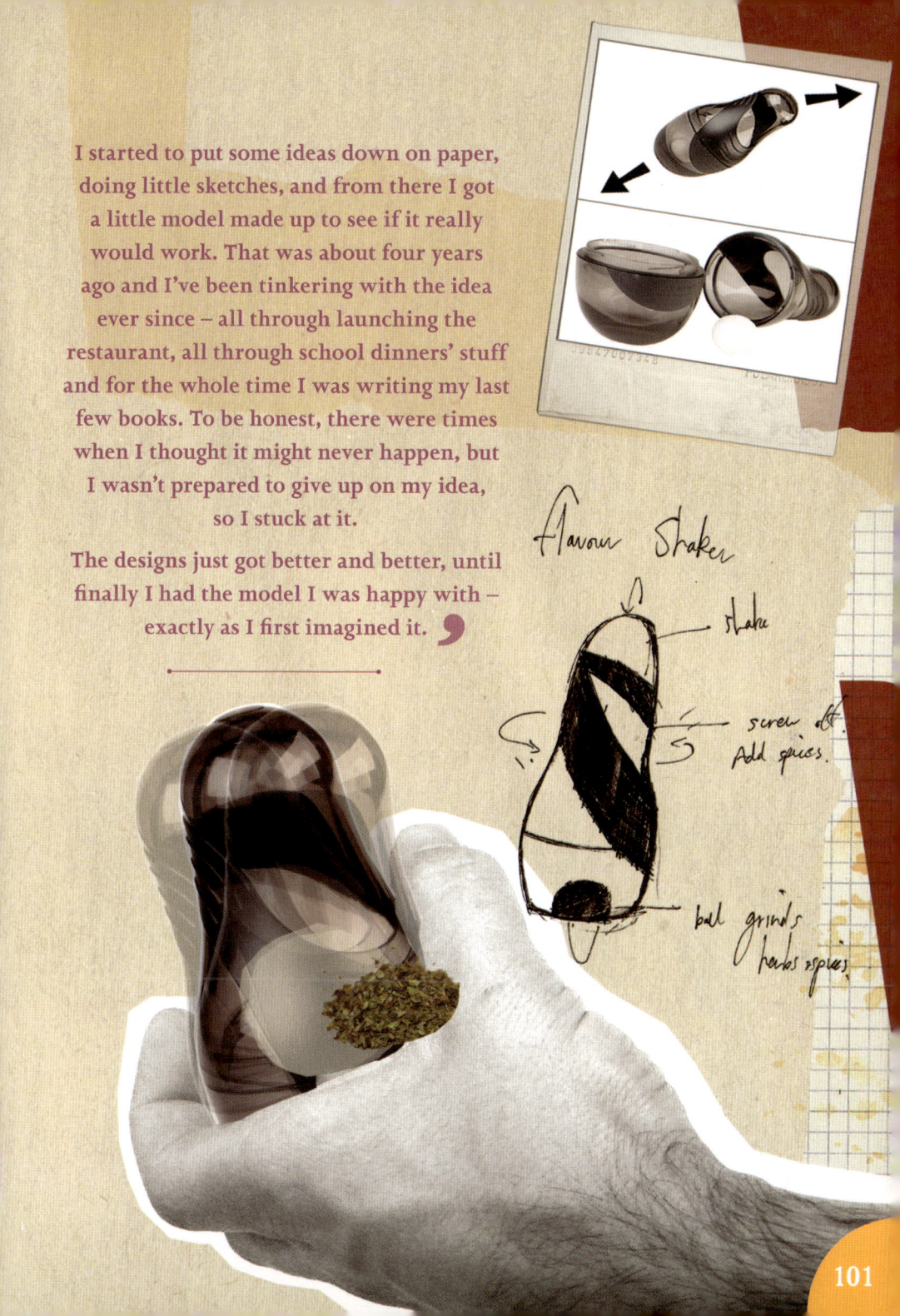

I started to put some ideas down on paper, doing little sketches, and from there I got a little model made up to see if it really would work. That was about four years ago and I've been tinkering with the idea ever since – all through launching the restaurant, all through school dinners' stuff and for the whole time I was writing my last few books. To be honest, there were times when I thought it might never happen, but I wasn't prepared to give up on my idea, so I stuck at it.

The designs just got better and better, until finally I had the model I was happy with – exactly as I first imagined it. **'**

Flavour Shaker

shake

screw off
Add spices

ball grinds herbs & spices

SHAKER SALES

Flavour Shakers are available in department stores across the UK and have been phenomenally successful. Since 2005, **A STAGGERING TWO MILLION HAVE BEEN SOLD IN MORE THAN FIFTEEN COUNTRIES AROUND THE WORLD**.

Jamie certainly seems to have the magic touch: his latest cookbook sold over 1.5 million copies in under six months, he launched an iPhone app that went straight to the top of the download chart, and his campaigns seem to catch the public imagination and reach the attention of politicians and policy makers.

IMPROVING THE WORLD AROUND YOU

If there is a formula to Jamie's success, it is that he has a track record of identifying problems and generating smart new solutions or responses to them. This is evident from the way he describes inventing the Flavour Shaker. He looks to improve the world around him, and in doing so creates useful ideas that seem to lead directly to his success.

> **JAMIE'S STYLE OF THINKING IS A TRAIT THAT HAS BEEN THE ORIGIN OF MANY OF THE WORLD'S MOST USEFUL INVENTIONS.**

For example, **POST-IT®** notes were invented by Arthur Fry when the page markers he used in his hymn book fell out and left him scrabbling for the right page. Fry's work for 3M gave him the idea to use one of their rejected weak adhesives to provide just enough stickiness to keep the markers in place, but not to rip the page when they are removed.

Another example is the **BALLPOINT PEN**, which was invented by a leather tanner called John Loud. Like Jamie, his invention was motivated by a problem encountered in his work; he needed a pen that would be able to write on the leather he tanned, which the then-common fountain pen couldn't do. His solution was to use a rotating steel ball at the nib, held in place by a socket. This quickly evolved to become the ubiquitous Biro.

What Jamie, Arthur Fry and John Loud have in common is the ability to spot and solve everyday problems and improvise until they have smart new solutions. **IT'S THE BEST SKILL AN INVENTOR CAN HAVE.**

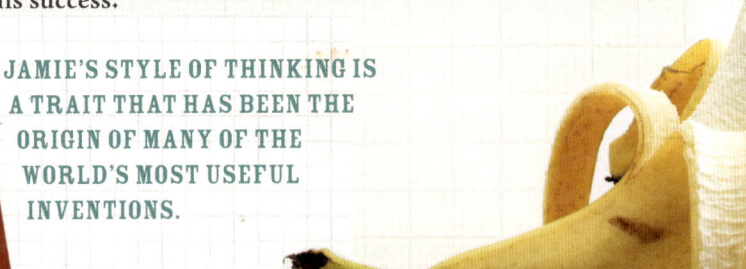

SHAKE YOUR OWN

Should you want to whip up a quick smoothie, but don't have a flavour shaker to hand, here's how to improvise your own using just a few household items.

Cut a large pear in half. Hollow out each side leaving about 1cm of flesh around the outsides.

Place the fruit selection gently into one half. Place the small unripe plum into the other half.

Now put the two halves of the pear together, holding them tightly between your hands and shake vigorously.

Ingredients
One large pear
One small unripe plum
One straw
For the fruit filling
50g Raspberries
50g Blueberries
¼ of a Banana
2 soft mango chunks

Clean your hands, face, body and walls if necessary.

Insert a straw into the side of the pear and enjoy.

HESTON BLUMENTHAL

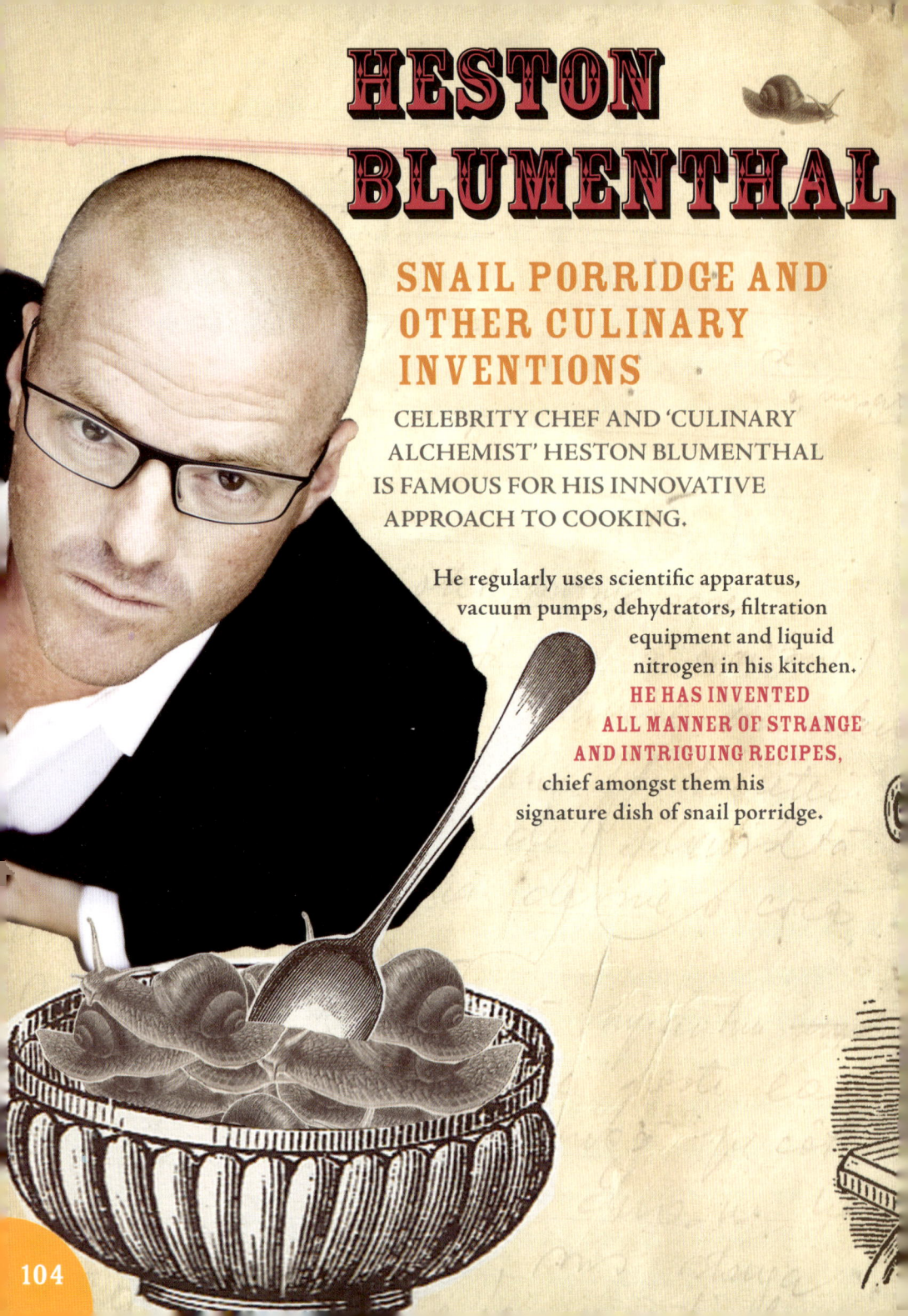

SNAIL PORRIDGE AND OTHER CULINARY INVENTIONS

CELEBRITY CHEF AND 'CULINARY ALCHEMIST' HESTON BLUMENTHAL IS FAMOUS FOR HIS INNOVATIVE APPROACH TO COOKING.

He regularly uses scientific apparatus, vacuum pumps, dehydrators, filtration equipment and liquid nitrogen in his kitchen. **HE HAS INVENTED ALL MANNER OF STRANGE AND INTRIGUING RECIPES,** chief amongst them his signature dish of snail porridge.

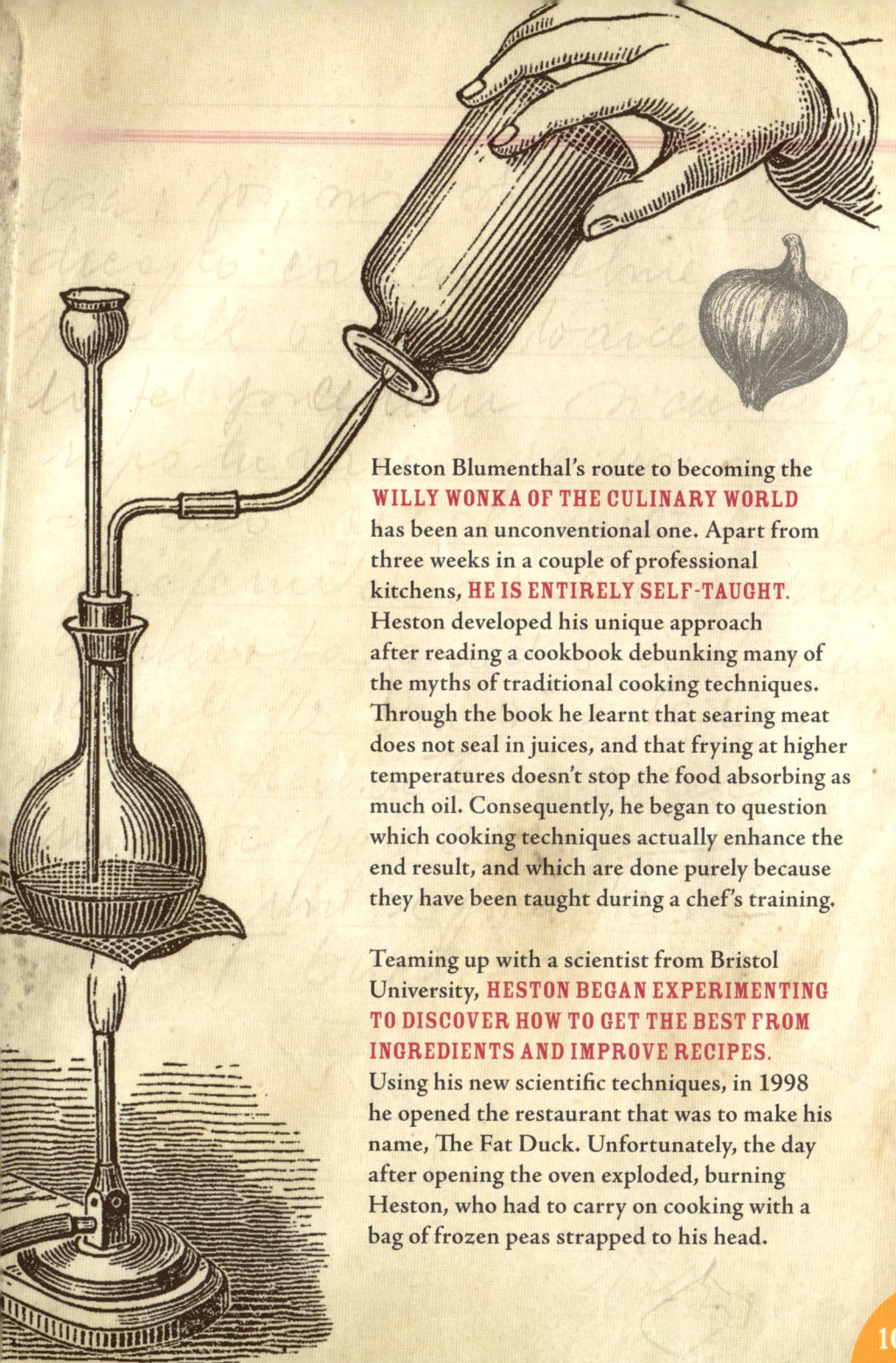

Heston Blumenthal's route to becoming the **WILLY WONKA OF THE CULINARY WORLD** has been an unconventional one. Apart from three weeks in a couple of professional kitchens, **HE IS ENTIRELY SELF-TAUGHT**. Heston developed his unique approach after reading a cookbook debunking many of the myths of traditional cooking techniques. Through the book he learnt that searing meat does not seal in juices, and that frying at higher temperatures doesn't stop the food absorbing as much oil. Consequently, he began to question which cooking techniques actually enhance the end result, and which are done purely because they have been taught during a chef's training.

Teaming up with a scientist from Bristol University, **HESTON BEGAN EXPERIMENTING TO DISCOVER HOW TO GET THE BEST FROM INGREDIENTS AND IMPROVE RECIPES**. Using his new scientific techniques, in 1998 he opened the restaurant that was to make his name, The Fat Duck. Unfortunately, the day after opening the oven exploded, burning Heston, who had to carry on cooking with a bag of frozen peas strapped to his head.

It was perhaps after a mild concussion that the idea for snail porridge occurred to him. He says the idea was inspired by taking the best of French cooking, mixing in one of the traditionally less appealing of Gallic ingredients and attempting to showcase his skills by making it appeal to the British palate.

If you can get over the name, **THE PORRIDGE IS SAID TO TASTE WONDERFUL.** He explains that to tempt diners to try it, the ingredients are all those that you might associate with snails, or that you would expect to marry with their flavour. The dish contains shallots, garlic, ham, parsley, butter, breakfast oats and sautéed snails, and takes 2–3 minutes to cook once the ingredients have been prepared. (The recipe is widely available should you want to try it for yourself.)

Initially Heston was worried that the dish might be perceived as grey and gloopy, and would prove unpopular, but in fact it has been tremendously successful. **THE WAITING LIST TO TRY IT AT THE FAT DUCK IS ALMOST SIX MONTHS LONG.**

CULINARY CREATIVITY

Alongside snail porridge, Heston has invented other bizarre culinary creations including bacon and egg ice cream, sardine on toast sorbet, salmon poached with liquorice and chocolate wine.

For his Channel 4 television series Heston took up the challenge of re-inventing some of the most bizarre dishes from history. His greatest results may be culinary masterpieces – but they don't sound entirely appetizing…

1. WHALE VOMIT STARTER: A dish from the Roman vomitarium, it's a starter that contains slivers of whale vomit, otherwise known as ambergris, which is a solid waxy substance produced by the digestive systems of sperm whales.

2. MEAT FRUIT: A dish invented by the Tudors, this consists of meat that is glazed and shaped to look like fruit, served in a fruit bowl.

3. MOCK TURTLE SOUP: A soup from the Victorian period that inspired a character in the Mad Hatter's Tea Party (and later a pop band). Turtle meat was expensive, so the soup is instead made from boiled cow's head.

4. DORMOUSE LOLLIPOPS: A version of a Roman dish, this is white-chocolate-coated dormouse paté, on a stick, served as a starter.

5. EJACULATING PUDDING: Inspired by the Roman God of Fertility, Priapus, the ejaculating pudding oozes juice when touched, and contains white chocolate mousse, 'space dust' popping candy and dry ice.

107

HARRY HOUDINI

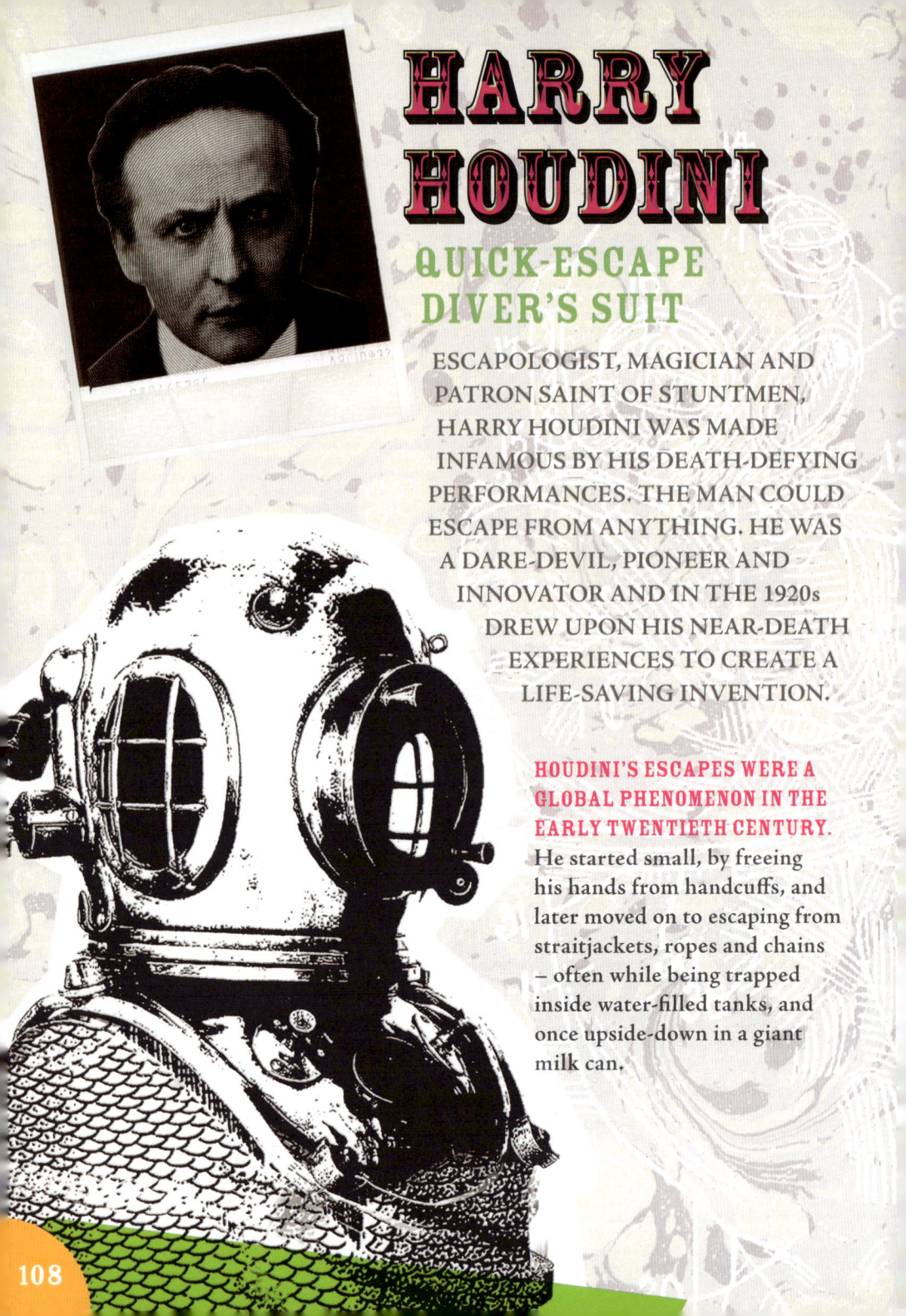

QUICK-ESCAPE DIVER'S SUIT

ESCAPOLOGIST, MAGICIAN AND PATRON SAINT OF STUNTMEN, HARRY HOUDINI WAS MADE INFAMOUS BY HIS DEATH-DEFYING PERFORMANCES. THE MAN COULD ESCAPE FROM ANYTHING. HE WAS A DARE-DEVIL, PIONEER AND INNOVATOR AND IN THE 1920s DREW UPON HIS NEAR-DEATH EXPERIENCES TO CREATE A LIFE-SAVING INVENTION.

HOUDINI'S ESCAPES WERE A GLOBAL PHENOMENON IN THE EARLY TWENTIETH CENTURY. He started small, by freeing his hands from handcuffs, and later moved on to escaping from straitjackets, ropes and chains – often while being trapped inside water-filled tanks, and once upside-down in a giant milk can.

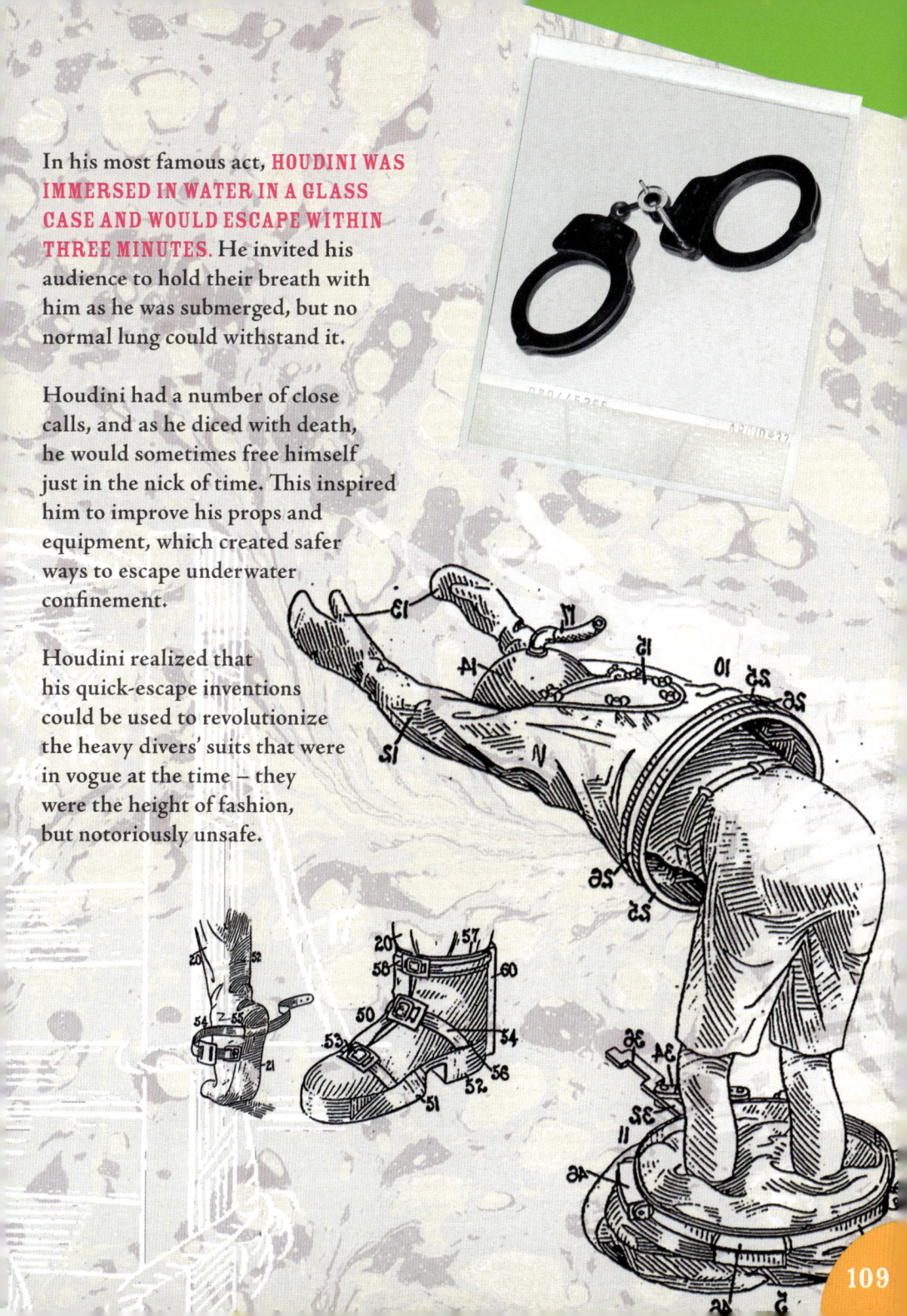

In his most famous act, **HOUDINI WAS IMMERSED IN WATER IN A GLASS CASE AND WOULD ESCAPE WITHIN THREE MINUTES.** He invited his audience to hold their breath with him as he was submerged, but no normal lung could withstand it.

Houdini had a number of close calls, and as he diced with death, he would sometimes free himself just in the nick of time. This inspired him to improve his props and equipment, which created safer ways to escape underwater confinement.

Houdini realized that his quick-escape inventions could be used to revolutionize the heavy divers' suits that were in vogue at the time — they were the height of fashion, but notoriously unsafe.

In 1921 Houdini filed a patent for a new type of diving suit. **IT ALLOWED THE DIVER TO GET OUT OF THE SUIT QUICKLY WHILE REMAINING UNDERWATER,** in case the air supply failed. It came in two halves, with a locking joint in the middle. In an emergency the diver could reach the joint, release it, and easily escape.

Much to Houdini's delight, the diving suit went on to save hundreds of lives.

PIONEERING SPIRIT

After filing his patent, Houdini continued to be an innovator and pioneer.

HE MADE ONE OF THE VERY FIRST VOICE RECORDINGS IN HISTORY using Edison's newly invented Phonograph. On them, he practises several different introductory speeches for his famous Chinese Water Torture Escape, and invites his sister Gladys to recite a poem.

He was also a **PIONEERING AVIATOR, AND PURCHASED ONE OF THE FIRST COMMERCIALLY AVAILABLE BIPLANES.** Despite limited flying experience, and having crashed in his initial attempts to take to the air, Houdini successfully completed the first powered flight ever made over Australia.

Throughout his life Houdini used his knowledge of innovative mechanisms and illusions to debunk and expose many of the spiritualists and fraudsters of the time, **DESPITE RECEIVING SEVERAL DEATH THREATS.**

It is ironic that after all his high-risk activities and escapes, Houdini's death came almost of his own volition after he invited a student, Gordon Whitehead, to punch him in the stomach to prove he would suffer no injury. Unfortunately, the blow led to a ruptured appendix, which killed him several days later.

CHARLEY BOORMAN

THE COLLAPSIBLE SHOVEL RAKE

ACTOR, INTREPID MOTORCYCLIST AND EXPLORER CHARLEY BOORMAN IS RENOWNED FOR THE EPIC JOURNEY ACROSS AFRICA HE UNDERTOOK WITH EWAN McGREGOR.

In fact, for years Charley has circumnavigated the globe using any means of travel available, **SLEEPING WHEREVER NATURE ALLOWED.** Inspired by these experiences, he has invented a product to make the life of the rugged traveller a bit more comfortable.

> Over the years I've had to kip in all sorts of places, out of necessity more than anything. I can't count the number of times I've wished that I had some sort of portable shovel-rake on me to make the ground more comfortable: it's so difficult to get it flat. I pick a spot, attempt to pat it down, then put the tent down – but every single time, no matter where I put my roll mat, there's a stone or something sticking up that I haven't seen.

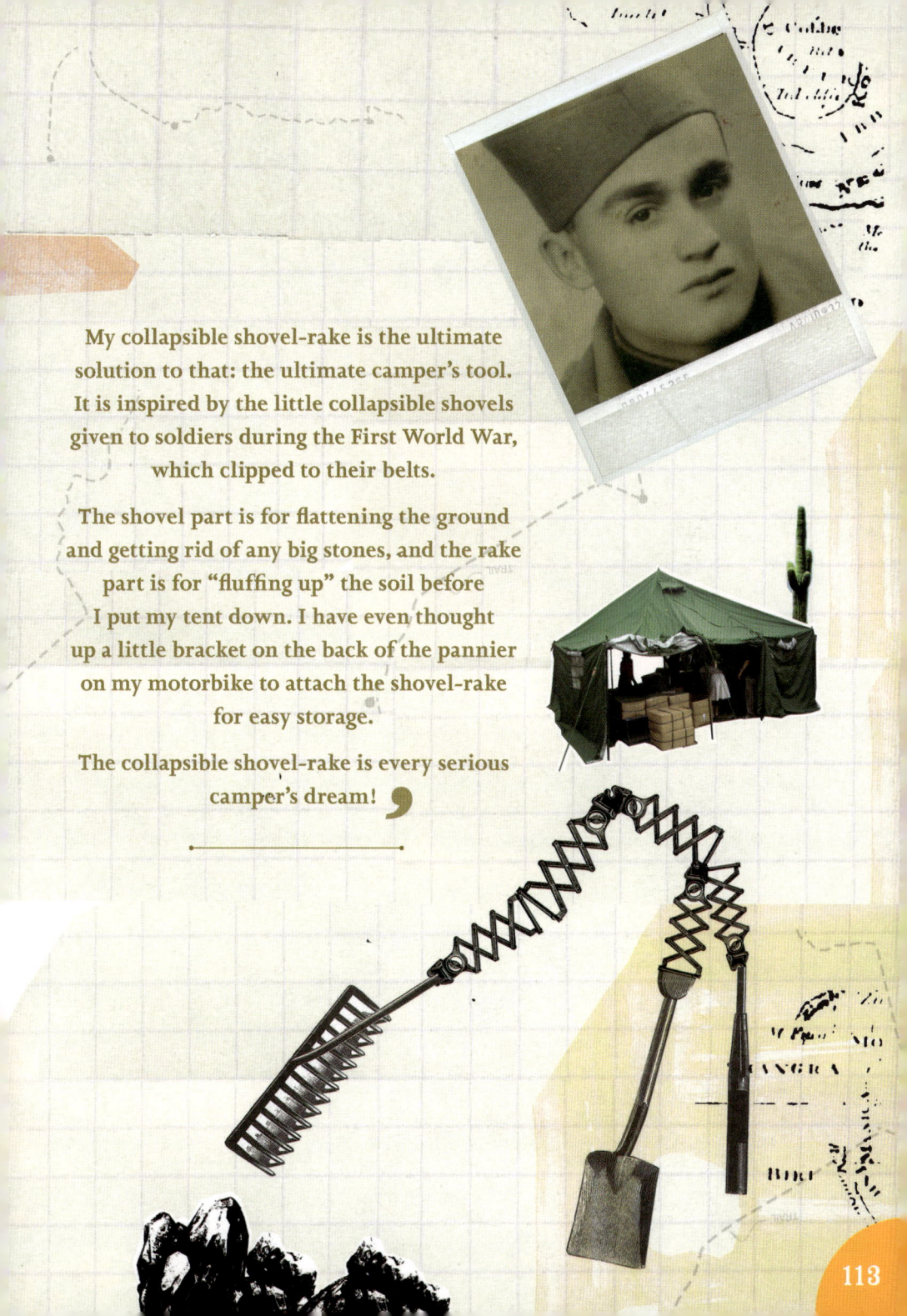

My collapsible shovel-rake is the ultimate solution to that: the ultimate camper's tool. It is inspired by the little collapsible shovels given to soldiers during the First World War, which clipped to their belts.

The shovel part is for flattening the ground and getting rid of any big stones, and the rake part is for "fluffing up" the soil before I put my tent down. I have even thought up a little bracket on the back of the pannier on my motorbike to attach the shovel-rake for easy storage.

The collapsible shovel-rake is every serious camper's dream! '

113

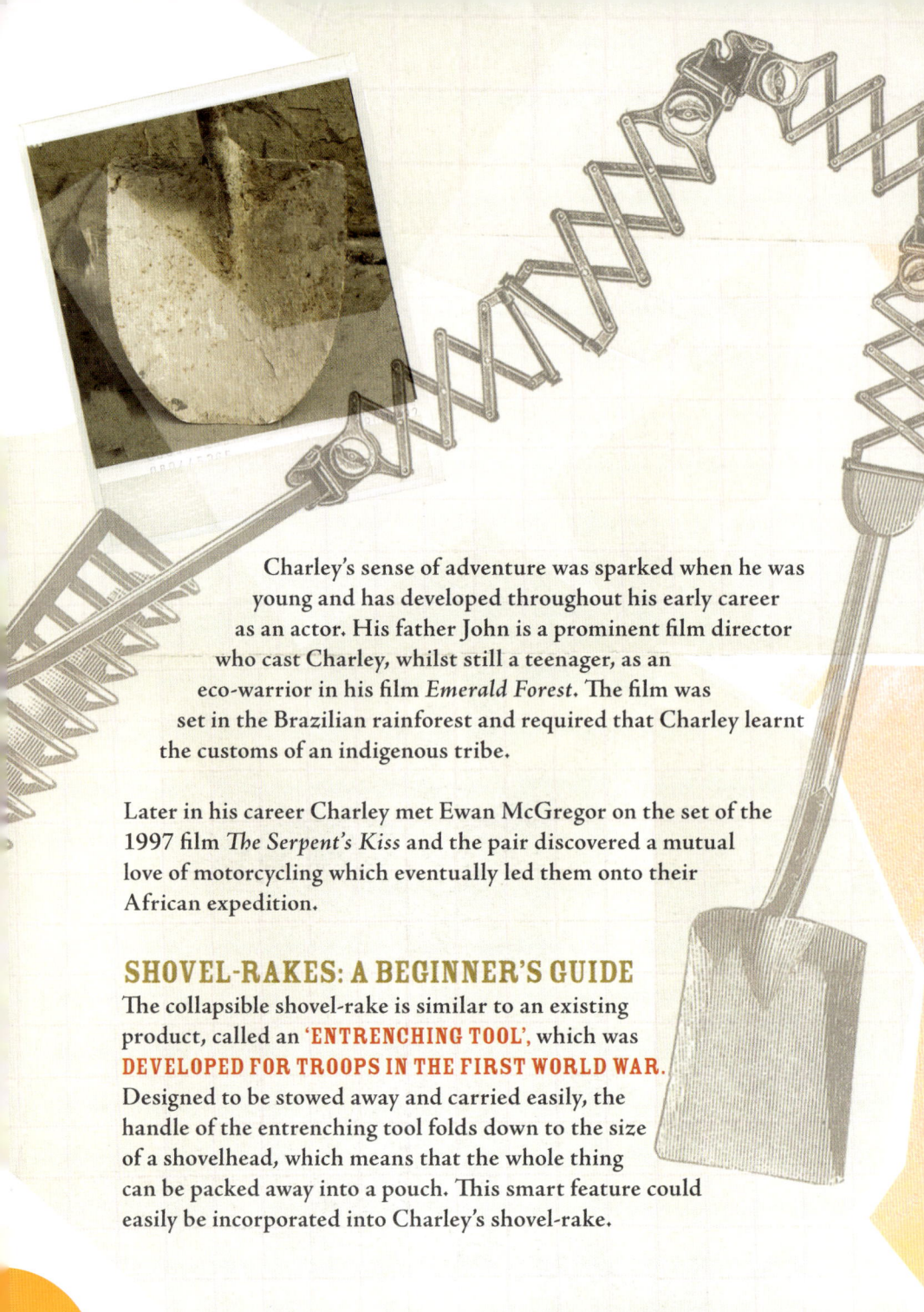

Charley's sense of adventure was sparked when he was young and has developed throughout his early career as an actor. His father John is a prominent film director who cast Charley, whilst still a teenager, as an eco-warrior in his film *Emerald Forest*. The film was set in the Brazilian rainforest and required that Charley learnt the customs of an indigenous tribe.

Later in his career Charley met Ewan McGregor on the set of the 1997 film *The Serpent's Kiss* and the pair discovered a mutual love of motorcycling which eventually led them onto their African expedition.

SHOVEL-RAKES: A BEGINNER'S GUIDE

The collapsible shovel-rake is similar to an existing product, called an **'ENTRENCHING TOOL'**, which was **DEVELOPED FOR TROOPS IN THE FIRST WORLD WAR.** Designed to be stowed away and carried easily, the handle of the entrenching tool folds down to the size of a shovelhead, which means that the whole thing can be packed away into a pouch. This smart feature could easily be incorporated into Charley's shovel-rake.

So this just leaves the question of how the 'rake' side of the shovel-rake would work. The best solution is to borrow the structure of a conventional lawn rake and made it durable enough to shovel up rocks and gravel.

By combining a lawn rake with an entrenching tool, **CHARLEY'S INVENTION COULD EASILY BE CREATED**. His ideal finishing touch would be a clip that attached the product to a motorcycle pannier, which would be simple enough to design.

CHARLEY'S IDEA REALLY COULD CHANGE THE WORLD OF THOUSANDS OF CAMPERS who, like Charley, could rest easy in the knowledge that, wherever their travels took them, they will always get a comfortable night's sleep at the end of the day.

URI GELLER

THE MONEYTRON, DIAMONTRON, GOLD METER (AND MANY MORE)

URI GELLER IS PERHAPS BEST KNOWN FOR BENDING CUTLERY USING ONLY THE POWER OF HIS MIND (AND POSSIBLY HIS THUMB). HE CLAIMS TO BE ABLE TO DEMONSTRATE SKILLS SUCH AS TELEPATHY, PSYCHOKINESIS, AND CAUSING SEEDS TO SPROUT WITH THE POWER OF HIS THOUGHTS. HE IS ALSO A PROLIFIC INVENTOR.

Whether Uri was victim of a series of expensive counterfeit scams is unknown, but in the early 1970s he certainly seemed to take the subject of expensive fakery very seriously. With a scientist friend Meir Gitlis, Uri invented the 'MONEYTRON' (which tells a fake banknote from a genuine one), the 'DIAMONTRON' (which detects fake diamonds) and the 'GOLD METER' (which, yes, you've guessed it, detects fake gold).

The devices are described as using an 'electro-chemical process controlled by a microcomputer' to determine fakery. All three devices are sold by Uri Geller Enterprises, and in press releases Uri describes the Moneytron as being 'bestselling'.

Not content with these inventions, Uri then turned his attention to safety equipment.

His next invention provides an early warning of earthquakes. It contains an array of pendulums that naturally react to vibrations. Uri says the device can distinguish between thunder, a sonic boom, a bomb or an earthquake, and will provide advance warning of a tremor that could mean the difference between life and death. The device has been installed in the elevators of the Azrieli Towers in Tel Aviv.

After tackling earthquakes, Uri registered a patent for a **GAS LEAK DETECTOR** that senses when gas in the air reaches dangerous levels, though this hasn't gone into commercial production.

A long-time advocate of the idea that our minds have untapped potential, Uri has suggested that **IN THE FUTURE IT MAY BE POSSIBLE TO CONTROL ALL KINDS OF DEVICES SUCH AS CARS OR COMPUTERS USING OUR THOUGHTS.** Geller's most recent invention is concerned with preserving our ability to do this; it is a shield against mobile phones, preventing electromagnetic waves from penetrating and potentially damaging the brain.

This brain-saving device is a metalized radiation shield that surrounds the phone like a mobile-phone case and deflects electromagnetic waves away from the head. However, due to the variety of shapes and sizes of phone available that do not fit his template, and repeated claims by manufacturers that their mobile technology is safe, his shield has not yet caught on commercially.

A THOUGHT-CONTROLLED FUTURE?

Uri's vision of a thought-controlled future sounds like science fiction but in fact could soon be a reality. An Austrian company, Guger Technologies, say they have almost perfected the **BRAIN-COMPUTER INTERFACE** (or BCI). The system measures fluctuations in electrical voltage in the brain and translates them into commands on a computer screen.

The BCI consists of a cap that fits over the user's head, with a few dozen holes through which electrodes are attached so that they rest on the scalp. The electrodes are connected via thin cables to a 'biosignal amplifier', which transmits the signals from the brain to a computer.

If fully developed the **BCI WOULD MAKE TYPING A THING OF THE PAST.** The invention would mean that people could simply think the words into a computer and they'd appear on the screen. Emails could be sent in a jiffy; documents could be written in the time it takes to think about them – in fact, people wouldn't have to sit in front of the computer at all! **THOUGHT CONTROL COULD REVOLUTIONIZE THE WAY WE LIVE.**

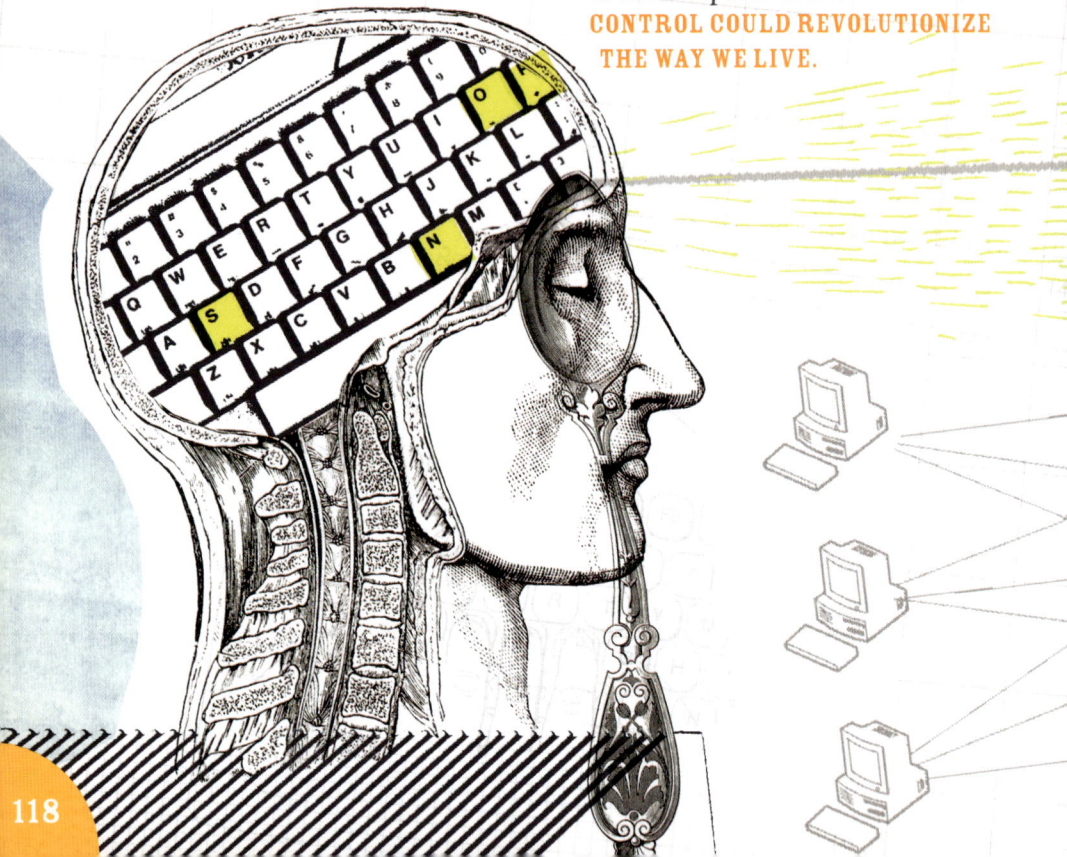

The Do's and Don'ts of using a thought-controlled computer at work

DO:
- Use it to transfer your thoughts directly into text on to your computer

DON'T:
- Use it in any situation when keeping your thoughts to yourself is preferable i.e. when you're around anyone you secretly fancy or if you really don't like your boss

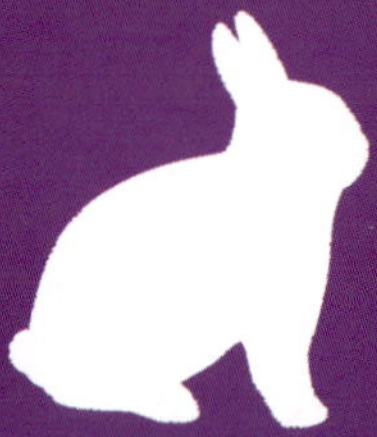

5. ARTISTS, DESIGNERS & WRITERS

ROALD DAHL

THE WADE-DAHL-TILL (WDT) BRAIN VALVE

MUCH-LOVED CHILDREN'S AUTHOR ROALD DAHL IS NO STRANGER WHEN IT COMES TO WEIRD AND WONDERFUL INVENTIONS. FROM EVERLASTING GOBSTOPPERS IN *CHARLIE AND THE CHOCOLATE FACTORY* TO *GEORGE'S MARVELLOUS MEDICINE*, DAHL'S VIVID STORYLINES AND OUT-OF-THIS-WORLD CHARACTERS HAVE DELIGHTED CHILDREN FOR DECADES.

But Roald's wildly creative mind was called to a more serious purpose in 1960 when his son Theo suffered a brain injury after being struck by a car. Desperate to speed up his son's recovery, **ROALD DEVOTED HIS ENERGIES TO CREATING A LIFESAVING NEW INVENTION** – the WDT brain valve.

Theo's injuries required regular draining of fluid from his brain using a tiny mechanical pump; however, the pump's valve regularly blocked up, causing him pain, blindness and the risk of permanent brain damage.

Witnessing his son's distress, **ROALD RESOLVED TO IMPROVE UPON THE CURRENT MEDICAL APPARATUS.** He enlisted the help of a friend and model-plane enthusiast, who supervised a factory producing precision hydraulic pumps, and teamed up with Theo's neurosurgeon to develop a new valve mechanism to improve the pump.

A HAPPY ENDING

The finished valve was, in fact, a tremendous success. The design comprised a clever mechanism that prevented blockages forming, and it was easy to fit and to clean.

It was introduced to the medical world in *The Lancet* medical journal in 1962 though, by the time it became available, Theo had recovered enough not to need it.

However, **SEVERAL THOUSAND OTHER CHILDREN HAVE BENEFITED** from the WDT valve, which has helped neurotechnology to progress in the years since.

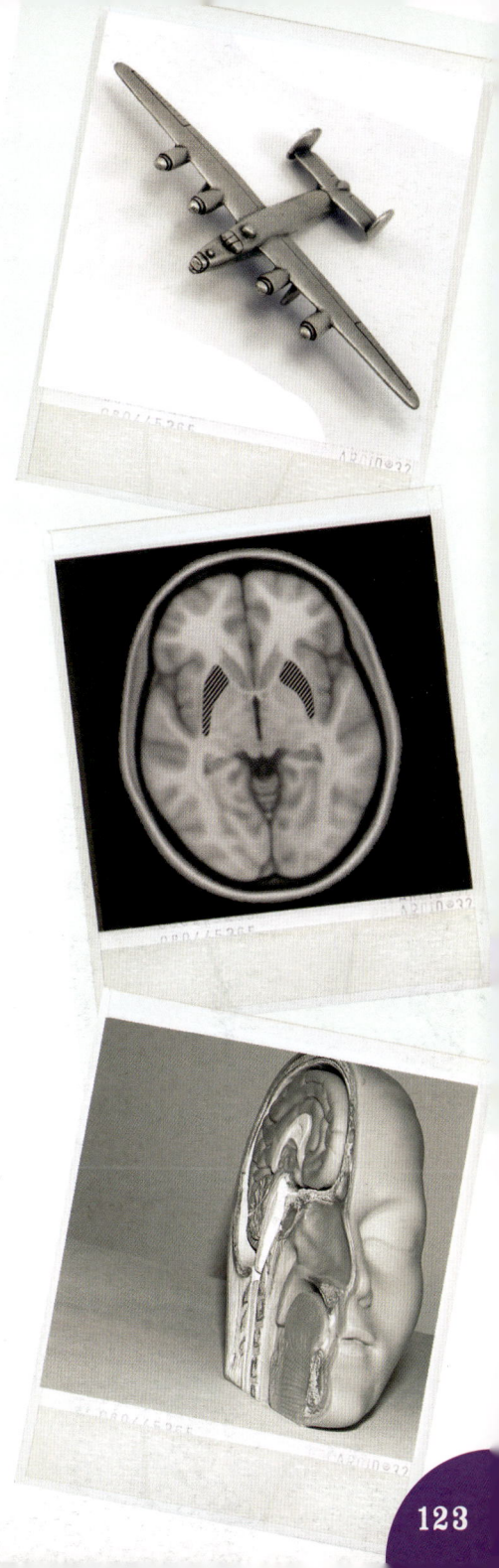

SWEET DREAMS!

Of course, not all of Roald Dahl's inventions were a matter of life or death. In fact, some of them could only exist in your wildest dreams! You only need to glance at Roald's most popular stories to see one of the world's most celebrated and untamed imaginations come to life. One of his most famous imaginative outlets was creating fantastical and incredible confectionery:

1. CAVITY-FILLING CARAMELS:
'no more dentists!'

2. TOFFEE-APPLE TREES:
for planting out in your garden

3. EDIBLE MARSHMALLOW PILLOWS:
for midnight feasts

4. MAGIC-HAND FUDGE:
'when you hold it in your hand, you taste it in your mouth!'

5. SCARLET SCORCHDROPPERS:
'makes the person who sucked them feel as warm as toast'

6. WRIGGLE-SWEETS:
'wriggle delightfully in your tummy after swallowing'

7. RAINBOW DROPS:
'suck them and you can spit in six different colours!'

8. HOT ICE CREAMS:
for cold days

9. LUMINOUS LOLLIES:
to eat at night

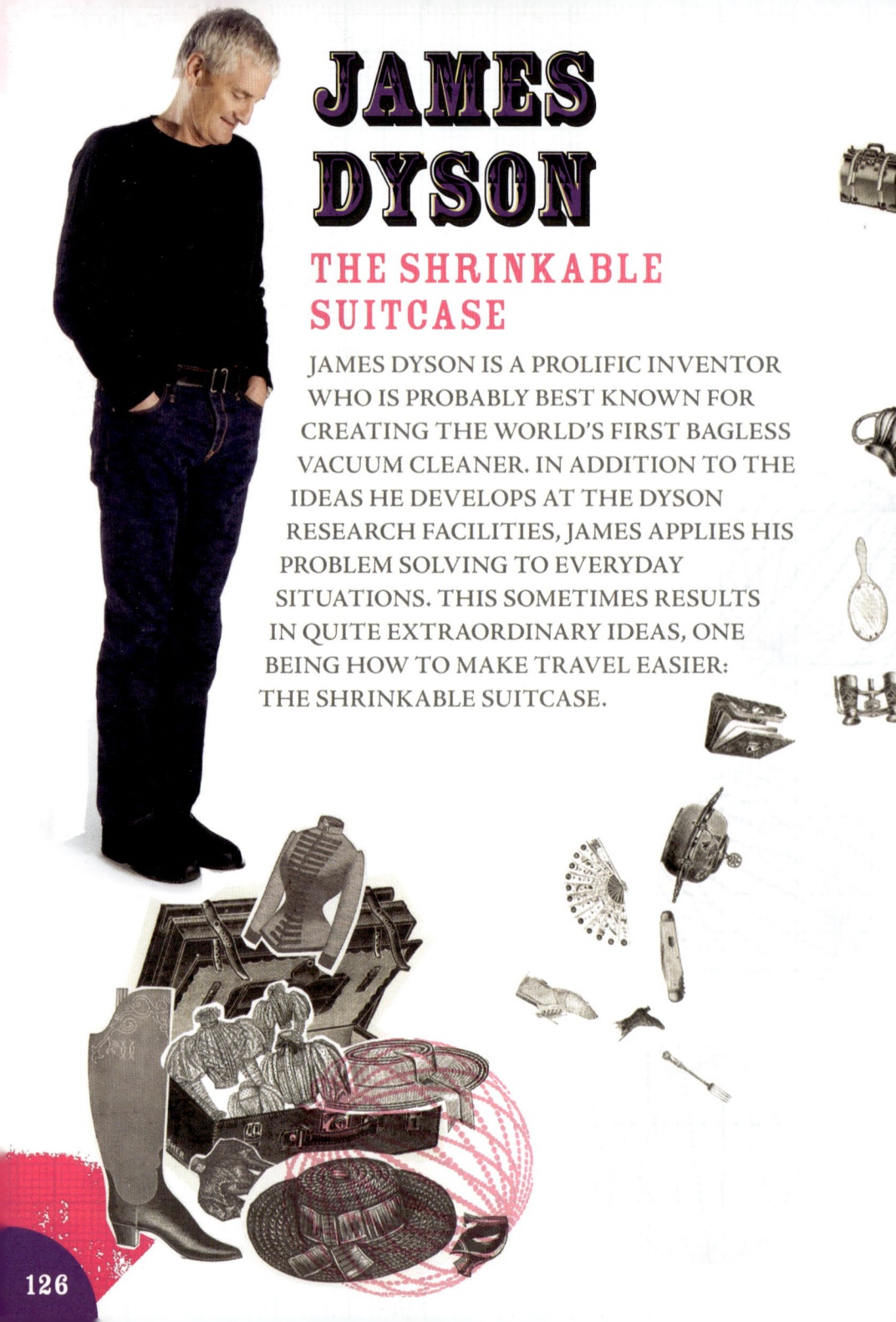

JAMES DYSON

THE SHRINKABLE SUITCASE

JAMES DYSON IS A PROLIFIC INVENTOR WHO IS PROBABLY BEST KNOWN FOR CREATING THE WORLD'S FIRST BAGLESS VACUUM CLEANER. IN ADDITION TO THE IDEAS HE DEVELOPS AT THE DYSON RESEARCH FACILITIES, JAMES APPLIES HIS PROBLEM SOLVING TO EVERYDAY SITUATIONS. THIS SOMETIMES RESULTS IN QUITE EXTRAORDINARY IDEAS, ONE BEING HOW TO MAKE TRAVEL EASIER: THE SHRINKABLE SUITCASE.

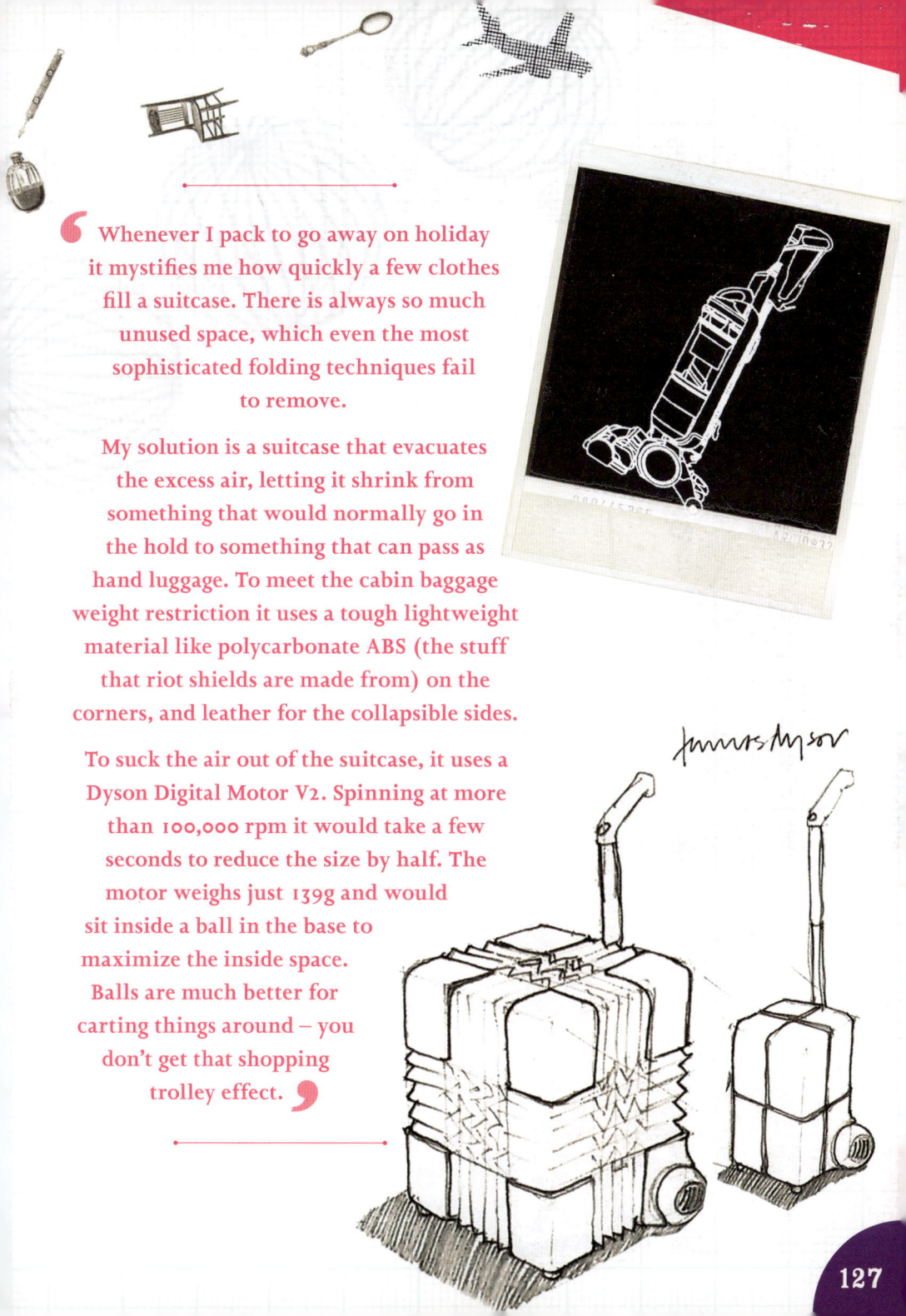

'Whenever I pack to go away on holiday it mystifies me how quickly a few clothes fill a suitcase. There is always so much unused space, which even the most sophisticated folding techniques fail to remove.

My solution is a suitcase that evacuates the excess air, letting it shrink from something that would normally go in the hold to something that can pass as hand luggage. To meet the cabin baggage weight restriction it uses a tough lightweight material like polycarbonate ABS (the stuff that riot shields are made from) on the corners, and leather for the collapsible sides.

To suck the air out of the suitcase, it uses a Dyson Digital Motor V2. Spinning at more than 100,000 rpm it would take a few seconds to reduce the size by half. The motor weighs just 139g and would sit inside a ball in the base to maximize the inside space. Balls are much better for carting things around – you don't get that shopping trolley effect.'

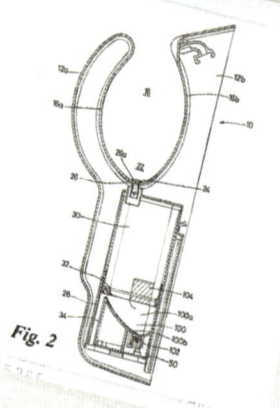

THE FERTILE MIND OF JAMES DYSON

Over the course of his career, James has developed a series of smart new solutions to everyday problems, and he is equally adept at investigating what further problems a particular solution may solve. The Shrinkable Suitcase is an abstract example, but James has come up with many others that have been developed and commercially launched.

One of James's earliest inventions solved the problem of how to make it easier to turn a wheelbarrow on uneven terrain and how to stop it sinking into the mud. His solution is elegant: **USE A BALL INSTEAD OF A WHEEL.** James realized that using a ball rather than wheels can be preferable in a range of situations, as a ball spreads weight over a wider area, and is easier to pivot around when turning – which is why he later incorporated one into his famous vacuum-cleaner design.

JAMES'S ICONIC BAGLESS VACUUM CLEANER WAS INSPIRED BY A TRIP TO A SAWMILL that made use of a huge cyclone vacuum to suck up sawdust. The cyclone vacuum doesn't require a filter or bag, and consequently doesn't lose suction as it picks up dust. Dyson saw the opportunity to scale down the same technology and use it in a vacuum-cleaner.

Fig. 2

Having developed the world's first 'no-loss-of-suction' vacuum cleaner, James and his team of engineers turned their minds to creating highly efficient digital motors to power Dyson machines. They discovered that when fast-moving air is channelled through a narrow slit (the thickness of an eyelash), it acts like a windscreen wiper, wiping the water off your hands.

So they created the **DYSON AIRBLADE™ HAND DRYER;** it was while refining this technology that the idea for the bladeless Air Multiplier™ fan was conceived.

With the **SHRINKABLE SUITCASE,** once again we see how his clever solutions can find new uses, with the spherical wheels and high-power motors being re-employed to create an innovative new product.

D'YOU KNOW WHAT HE SHOULD MAKE...?

The next big Dyson product:

Airblade™ Dryer Doorways: Could Dyson's hand dryer be scaled up to dry a whole person, either entering a building out of the rain, or perhaps stepping out of the shower?

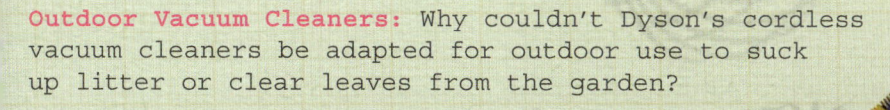

Outdoor Vacuum Cleaners: Why couldn't Dyson's cordless vacuum cleaners be adapted for outdoor use to suck up litter or clear leaves from the garden?

Shrinkable Bins: Using the same principle as the shrinkable suitcase, household rubbish bins could compress and shrink-wrap waste. This would also stop smells escaping and help solve the issue of finding enough landfill space.

ANDY WARHOL

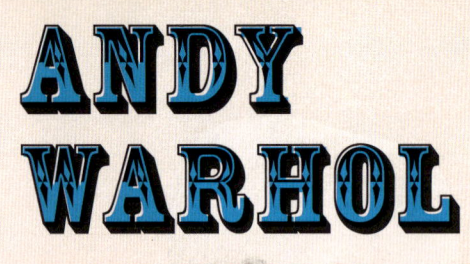

FIVE-FACED WATCH

ARTIST ANDY WARHOL IS ONE OF ONLY SIX ARTISTS WHOSE WORK HAS SOLD FOR OVER $100 MILLION. AS A KEY FOUNDER OF THE POP ART MOVEMENT, ANDY IS PROBABLY BEST KNOWN FOR HIS COLOURFUL SCREEN PRINTS OF ICONIC CELEBRITIES SUCH AS MARILYN MONROE, ELVIS AND THE QUEEN.

He also dabbled as an inventor, creating an intriguing mechanism with an equally intriguing story behind it…

Andy was an eccentric bohemian, with a flamboyant appearance and an equally flamboyant lifestyle. In 1962 he set up 'The Factory', which was his studio, and doubled as a place to hang out for a menagerie of artists, drag queens, musicians and free-thinkers who supported and influenced his work.

Andy experimented with new ideas for film, music and publishing. He founded *Interview* magazine and managed **THE VELVET UNDERGROUND**, a 1960s experimental rock band, and it was during this period that he also tried his hand at inventing.

Whilst living in New York, Andy produced sketches for an interesting adaptation to an everyday object, creating the **'FIVE-FACED WATCH'**. Instead of having a strap, the watch was entirely comprised of interlinked watch faces.

The sketches did not come to light during his lifetime; however, two years after his death in 1987, the executor of his estate found, refined and patented the designs, with the collaboration of the North American Watch Company.

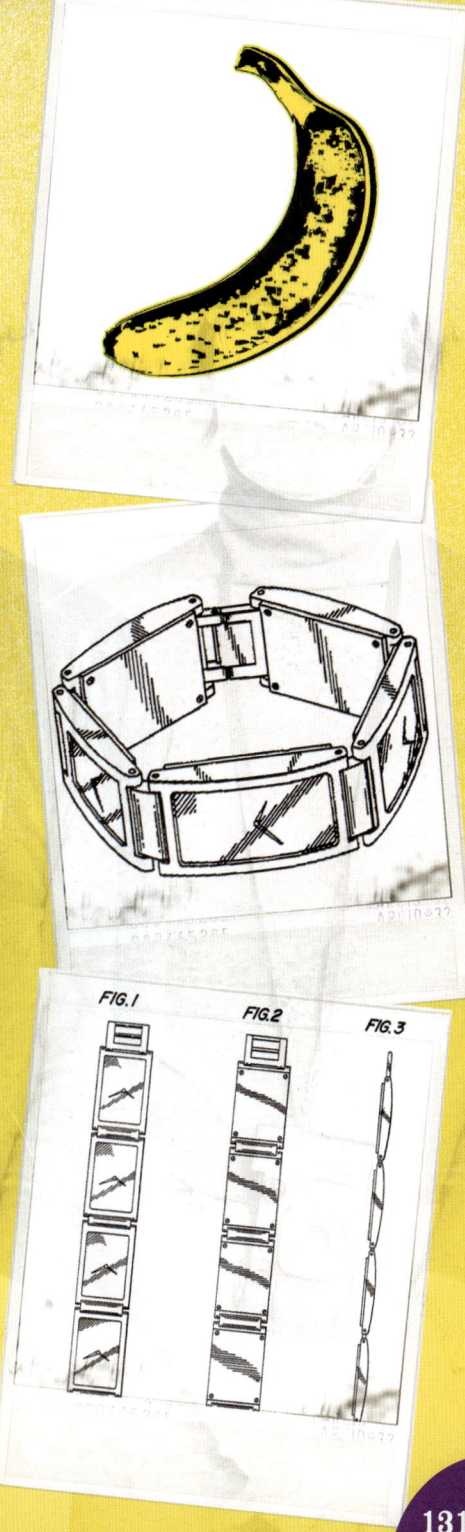

SECRETS AND SPIES: THE STORY BEHIND THE IDEA

Since it was posthumously filed, the patent submitted does not describe the thinking behind the invention. It may have been that the design simply appealed to Warhol's aesthetic sense; he was keen on repetition, as his multiple prints demonstrate. Equally, the watch may also have had a practical intention. As an international traveller and businessman, Andy may have designed it so **HE COULD SET EACH WATCH FACE TO KEEP TRACK OF THE TIME IN THE KEY CITIES OF THE WORLD.** This would certainly have been useful to the jet-setter businessman of the 1970s and 80s. In fact, watches with multiple faces are now commercially available for just such a purpose.

One other explanation regards an attempt on his life. In 1968, Valerie Solanas shot Andy three times in the chest. He survived the attack, and perhaps understandably became more concerned with surveillance and security. As a result, **HE BEGAN TO DEVELOP AN INTEREST IN THE SPYING AND SURVEILLANCE GADGETS** used during the war, and by private detectives at the time. Inspired by coat-button cameras, secret transmitters and hidden microphones, the watch may have been a result of his interest in surveillance art and the ingenious adaptation of everyday objects so important to the surveillance industry.

INTRIGUING SPYING GADGETS UNCOVERED IN THE 1960s

1. THE EXPLODING CHOCOLATE BAR: Developed by the Germans during the Second World War, it's made of steel with a thin covering of real chocolate. When the piece of chocolate at the end is broken, a strip of canvas is pulled out and within seconds the bomb explodes.

2. DOG POO TRANSMITTER: Fake dog poo with transmitters inside were used in the streets of Russia and the US during the Cold War. The transmitters were also used in the Vietnam War to mark targets.

3. OLIVE MICROPHONE:
A microphone disguised as an olive was used by American private detectives in the 1960s to record conversations. The device was placed in a vodka Martini, with the toothpick acting as an antenna. The device works well as long as it isn't eaten.

ORLA KIELY

THE WOTTLE

ORLA KIELY IS AN IRISH FASHION DESIGNER PERHAPS BEST KNOWN FOR HER DISTINCTIVE PRINTS WHICH ADORN CLOTHES, BAGS, ACCESSORIES AND EVEN WELLIES. AS A KEEN RECYCLER, ORLA RECENTLY TURNED HER ATTENTION TO CREATING A SOLUTION FOR THE VAST QUANTITIES OF DISPOSABLE BOTTLES THAT CLOG LANDFILL SITES ACROSS THE COUNTRY.

> I have two kids and I recognize the need to keep them well hydrated, so I make sure they have plenty of water to drink when they are out or at school.
>
> However, I think using a plastic mineral water bottle only once is ridiculous. In the past I had been refilling old bottles to give to my children, but I wasn't confident about how hygienic this was and I worried when I heard that certain plastics can leach into the water. Plastic mineral-water bottles are very clear that they are one-use only.

So I decided to work on an idea called the Wottle. It is a desirable, safe, recycled and reusable alternative to the disposable bottle. The idea is to regularly fill up your Wottle, preferably with filtered tap water, to help reduce the amount of landfill we create using disposable bottles.

I love that you can go into a restaurant and you're now asked "sparkling, still or tap?" The thinking has changed: we're much more aware about landfill. It used to be that mineral water was considered better than tap. Hurrah!

The Wottle has been launched and is now widely available. I'm delighted that it is making a difference. ,

Described by the *Guardian* as 'the Queen of Prints', Orla credits her grandmother as being the creative inspiration in her life. For the Wottle, once again, she took inspiration from her family, in this case her sons, and has created a product intended to make the world a better place for the next generation.

The Wottle has been selling well in the UK since 2008. It is manufactured in Suffolk from **100% RECYCLED BPA-FREE PLASTIC** and provides a green alternative to disposable water bottles.

DISPOSABLE BOTTLES: A PROBLEM THAT NEEDS SOLVING

As Orla advocates, there are plenty of reasons why drinking tap water in refillable bottles is preferable. For a start, it'll cost us less. **BRITAIN CONSUMES 3 BILLION LITRES OF BOTTLED WATER PER YEAR.** Typically the price of bottled water is 500 times more expensive than the price of tap water.

Then there are the resources it consumes. Each year **IN THE UK WE THROW AWAY ALMOST 10 BILLION DISPOSABLE BOTTLES.** Worldwide, the amount of oil used to produce disposable bottles each year (17 million barrels) could fuel over 1,000,000 cars for an entire year. It is also reckoned that it takes three bottles of water to make and distribute *one* disposable plastic bottle of water.

Finally, as Orla explains, there's the waste that is created, as **80% OF ALL DISPOSABLE BOTTLES AREN'T RECYCLED;** most go to landfill, where it could take over 500 years for the bottles to degrade. Equally, many 'discarded' bottles become environmental pollution and can be found in hedgerows, parks, streams and rivers. Via rivers they can be transported to the open seas. The Eastern Garbage Patch is a floating area of waste plastic in the Pacific Ocean, six times the size of England. It is the world's largest waste dump, and drastically affects animals and ecosystems that come into contact with it.

There are plenty of reasons to use a refillable bottle, and Orla's practical and beautiful Wottle gives us another one.

WALT DISNEY

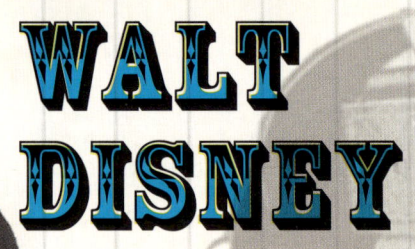

THE SHADOW PROJECTOR

WALT DISNEY REMAINS THE MOST SUCCESSFUL ANIMATOR OF ALL TIME. THE DISNEY CORPORATION IS THE LARGEST MEDIA AND ENTERTAINMENT COMPANY IN THE WORLD, COMPRISING EVERYTHING FROM THEME PARKS TO SHOPS.

But starting out, Walt's success was far from assured, and he gambled everything on the success of a film that made use of a new invention, **ONE THAT WAS TO REVOLUTIONIZE ANIMATION.**

When Walt's career took off in the early 1930s, animation was relatively unsophisticated, featuring flat-looking cartoon characters moving in front of a stationary, unchanging background.

Animators found it difficult to advance beyond this stage as it was time consuming and complicated to create realistic-looking, moving backgrounds, and accurately represent how a character's shadow would fall. **WALT DISNEY SAW THIS PROBLEM AS AN OPPORTUNITY** and began developing pioneering animation techniques.

His breakthrough came with the invention of his **SHADOW PROJECTOR,** which enabled the animator to see exactly how the shadow should be drawn to create a lifelike effect. Walt's device incorporated a lamp that could be positioned to replicate the animator's desired light source against the scene background. This way the animator could draw a perfectly realistic shadow for every frame.

THE GAMBLE...

Walt's invention provided a technological leap forward that enabled cartoons to appear more life-like and engaging, and this led to Walt's gamble.

At the time, no one had made a feature-length cartoon as it was believed that an animation would not be able to capture people's attention for long periods. **HAVING DEVELOPED HIS NEW INVENTION, WALT THOUGHT DIFFERENTLY.** In 1934 he decided to make *Snow White and the Seven Dwarfs*, an animated story based upon a Grimm brothers' fairy tale. Both his brother and wife attempted to talk him out of going ahead with the project, but he was so confident in the story and his new invention that **HE EVEN MORTGAGED HIS HOUSE TO FINANCE IT.**

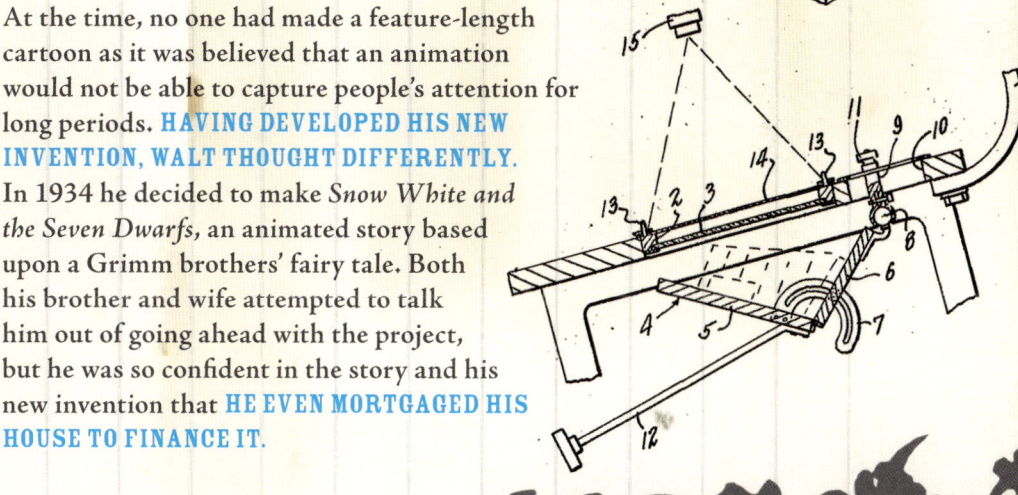

THE PAY-OFF...

It took Walt three years to make the film, and in December 1937 it premiered to great acclaim. **BY 1939 IT HAD BECOME THE HIGHEST-GROSSING FILM IN HISTORY.** With the profits, Walt established the Disney studio complex in California and followed up his success with films such as *Pinocchio* and *Dumbo*. Even now, *Snow White and the Seven Dwarfs* is one of the highest-grossing films ever. Quite a pay-off for his gamble.

It is worth re-watching the film to see the influence of his invention. You'll notice that scenes are set in difficult low-lighting conditions, for example by candlelight, and have complicated backgrounds, such as woodland. The shadows in the film are almost over-emphasized, showing off Walt's new technique and groundbreaking, money-making invention.

SNOW WHITE AND THE OTHER DWARFS

Alongside his new shadow projector invention, Walt stated that, for him, the success of the film relied upon the engaging characters of the Seven Dwarfs, and 'their possibilities for "screwiness" and "gags"'.

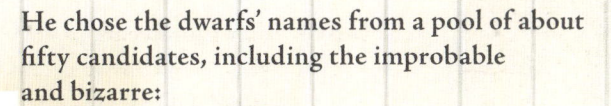

He chose the dwarfs' names from a pool of about fifty candidates, including the improbable and bizarre:

JUMPY	**BALDY**	**PUFFY**
DEAFY	**NIFTY**	**STUFFY**
DIZZEY	**SNIFFY**	**TUBBY**
HICKEY	**SWIFT**	**SHORTY**
WHEEZY	**LAZY**	**BURPY**

DONATELLA VERSACE

ASYMMETRIC PEN

ITALIAN DESIGNER DONATELLA VERSACE IS VICE-PRESIDENT OF THE FASHION COMPANY VERSACE AND CHIEF DESIGNER OF ITS CURRENT LINE OF CLOTHING.

Most famous for creating iconic outfits for red-carpet events, Donatella has recently branched out in a new direction and tried her hand at invention, registering a design for an intriguing **'ASYMMETRIC PEN'** to address a personal issue she has had been burdened with since childhood.

Donatella grew up in Italy and started her career in marketing before being convinced to try fashion design in the early 1970s. With her instinct for PR, **DONATELLA WAS ONE OF THE FIRST DESIGNERS TO CAPITALIZE ON THE LINK BETWEEN FASHION AND CELEBRITY,** creating clothes for Madonna, Elizabeth Hurley and Princess Diana, amongst others. She is associated with flamboyant prints and over-the-top sexuality, and her most famous garment, nicknamed the 'Jungle Dress', was a green chiffon dress that (barely) clung to Jennifer Lopez at the Emmy Awards in 2000. **IT IS BELIEVED TO BE THE MOST PHOTOGRAPHED DRESS IN HISTORY.**

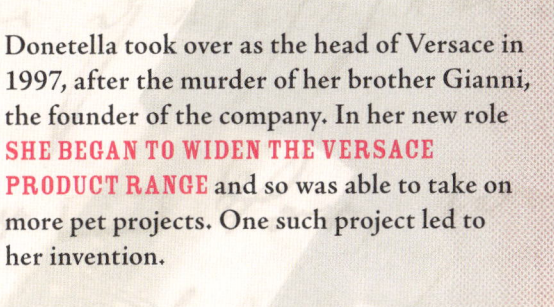

Donetella took over as the head of Versace in 1997, after the murder of her brother Gianni, the founder of the company. In her new role **SHE BEGAN TO WIDEN THE VERSACE PRODUCT RANGE** and so was able to take on more pet projects. One such project led to her invention.

From a young age, Donatella had developed a highly distinctive and unusual handwriting style. She holds a pen between her thumb, first and middle fingers, as is conventional, but then tucks her middle finger under the pen. The consequence is that the pen is angled oddly against the paper, which, when using a ballpoint, often leads to the flow of ink blocking. In 2000, she registered a design for a pen that solved the problem.

143

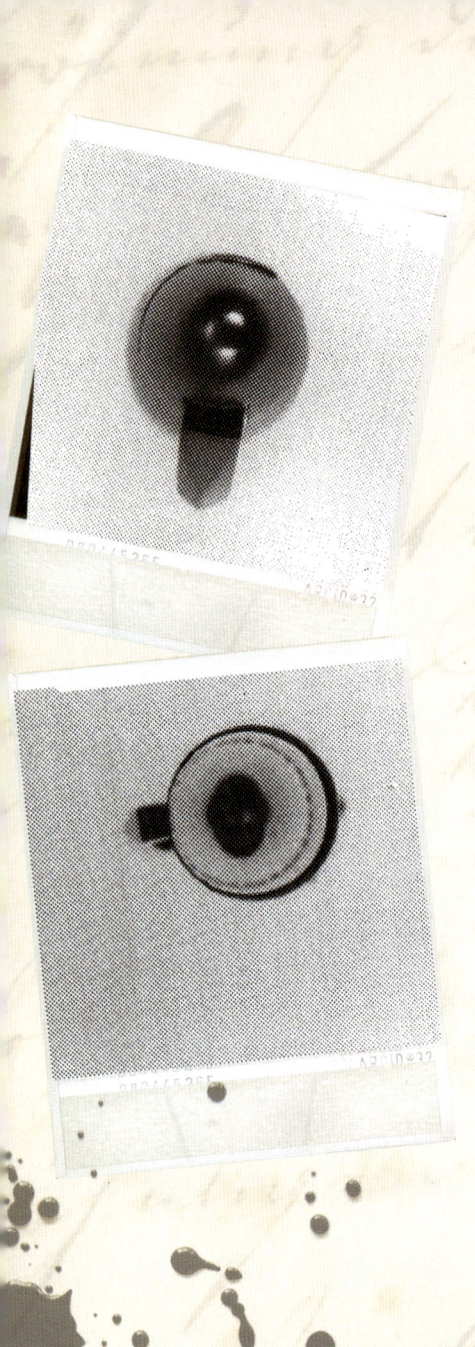

A SIGNATURE SOLUTION

At first glance her asymmetric design looks perfectly normal; however, her pen tapers off to one side, such that the point of the pen is not vertically beneath the top. In effect, the ballpoint refill inside the pen does not run through the centre, but is angled slightly so that the point emerges to one side. This means that, when used, the point of the pen will be at a less acute angle, and will therefore function much more effectively than a normal ballpoint pen.

As is fitting for a fashion designer, **DONATELLA HAS ADDED HER OWN FLOURISHES AND SIGNATURE STYLE TO THE PEN**, incorporating gold trim and diagonal slashes at the top and side of the pen.

Stationery seems like an odd area for Versace to expand into, which is perhaps why, as yet, **DONATELLA HAS NOT COMMERCIALIZED THE PEN.** Only a limited number of the pens have been made, and they are confined, for the moment, to her own use.

Perhaps, as with her fashion wear, she is looking for an endorsement by a celebrity with particularly beautiful hands to show off a new range of Versace pens to their best effect.

INNOVATIVE FASHION

Should Donetella want to bring a similar level of functional innovation to her latest fashion wear, she need look no further than the patent office. Its archive contains a wealth of intriguing and bizarre patents for clothing.

1. AIR-CONDITIONED SHIRT: A shirt that inflates with cold air from a built-in air-con.

2. THE TOWELCHO: Half towel, half poncho – a towel with a head-sized hole in the middle designed for use at the beach.

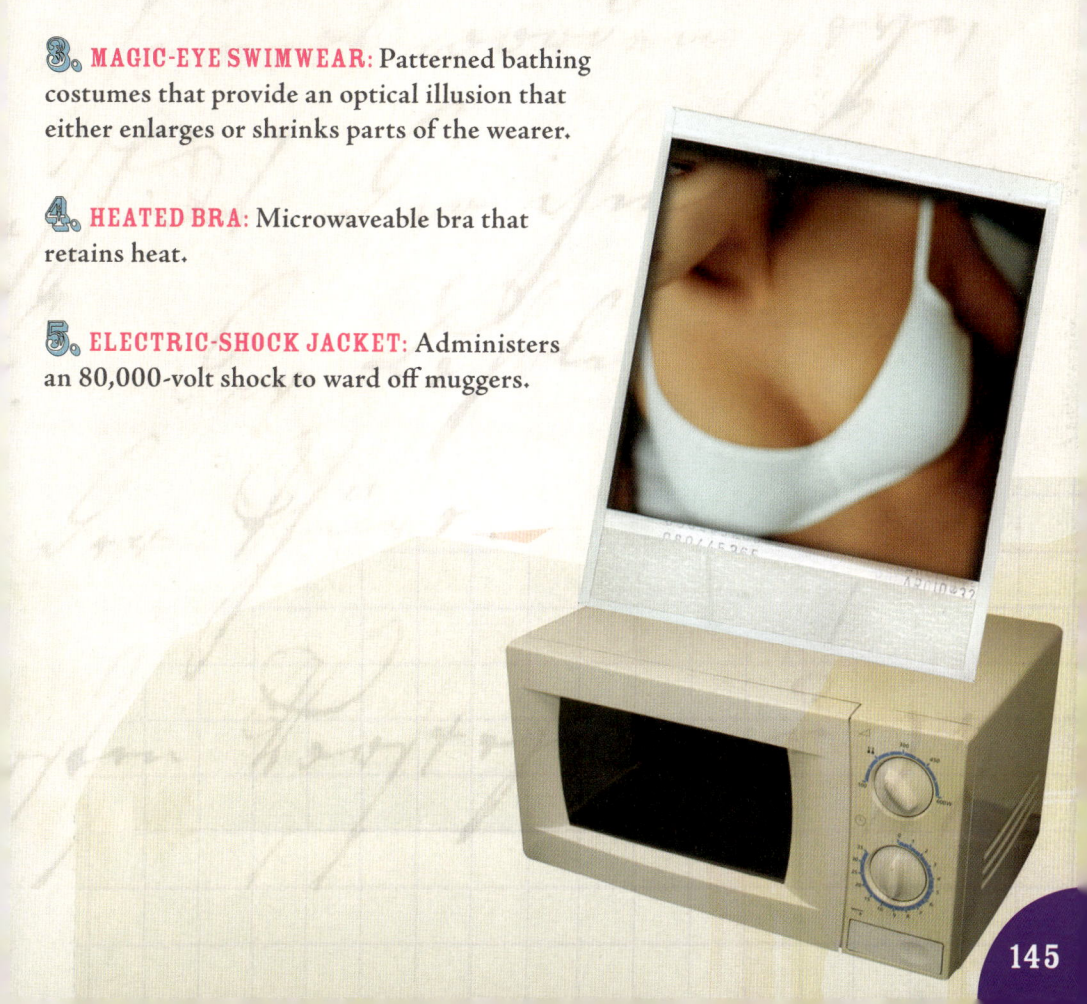

3. MAGIC-EYE SWIMWEAR: Patterned bathing costumes that provide an optical illusion that either enlarges or shrinks parts of the wearer.

4. HEATED BRA: Microwaveable bra that retains heat.

5. ELECTRIC-SHOCK JACKET: Administers an 80,000-volt shock to ward off muggers.

MARK TWAIN
SELF-PASTING SCRAPBOOK

UNBEKNOWNST TO MANY, MARK TWAIN, THE AMERICAN HUMOURIST AND AUTHOR OF *ADVENTURES OF HUCKLEBERRY FINN*, WAS FASCINATED BY SCIENCE AND KEEN ON INNOVATION.

Keeping up with the foremost thinkers and inventors of the day, he developed friendships with business pioneers, artists and industrialists, and dabbled in all these fields himself.

In the mid-nineteenth century, Twain patented three inventions. The first, **A MECHANISM TO REPLACE TROUSER BRACES**, fell by the wayside. The second, the aptly named **'HISTORY TRIVIA BOARD GAME'**, also remained consigned to history. But the third, and final, invention by this literary heavyweight was the most ingenious of them all – **THE SELF-PASTING SCRAPBOOK**.

Twain kept a series of scrapbooks that recorded his journeys across America. They were brimming with pictures, photographs and artefacts that he collected along the way. At the time, since Pritt Stick hadn't been invented, the only means of fixing these items into a scrapbook was to use a pot of glue and a brush, but Twain found that carrying these items around was a bit of a nuisance, and the process of carefully applying glue to the back of objects while travelling was impractical and often messy. So, in a burst of admirable insight, **TWAIN'S SOLUTION WAS TO PRODUCE SCRAPBOOKS WITH THE GLUE ALREADY APPLIED,** in a dried strip running though the centre of every page.

GLUE HERE

DID THE IDEA STICK?

When it was patented in 1872, the Self-Pasting Scrapbook was immediately successful. **IT CHANGED THE WAY PEOPLE THOUGHT ABOUT GLUE,** paving the way for Pritt Stick, sticky tape, Post-it® notes and so on. Even today, photo albums and scrapbooks use self-pasting pages.

Thanks partly to Mark's invention, **'SCRAPBOOKING' IS NOW BIG BUSINESS,** particularly in the US. The industry is estimated to be worth over $3 billion, with 1,600 companies producing 'scrapbooking' products and 25 million Americans considering themselves 'scrapbookers'.

Mark Twain was not alone in his love of all things scrappy. Some well-known scrapbookers include Queen Victoria and US presidents Thomas Jefferson and Rutherford B. Hayes. Andy Warhol also had an obsession with collecting things and during his teenage years made used one of Mark Twain's self-pasting scrapbooks to collect photographs of movie stars. It was in this very scrapbook that he is said to have coined his most famous phrase: **'IN THE FUTURE, EVERYONE WILL BE WORLD-FAMOUS FOR 15 MINUTES.'**

In the words of Mark Twain...

- "Be careful about reading health books. You may die of a misprint."
- Supposing is good, but finding out is better.
- A cauliflower is nothing but a cabbage with a college education.
- Accident is the name of the greatest of all inventors.
- A person with a new idea is a crank until the new idea succeeds!!

PAUL SMITH

THE BUNNY BIN

BRITISH FASHION DESIGNER SIR PAUL SMITH IS MOST FAMOUS FOR HIS TAILORED SUITS AND SIGNATURE MULTI-STRIPE PATTERN, WHICH HAS ADORNED EVERYTHING FROM SHIRTS TO PERFUME BOTTLES, AND FROM CUFFLINKS TO MINIS. ALONGSIDE HIS PASSION FOR FASHION, PAUL HAS A LIFELONG, UNRELATED, AMBITION: TO KEEP BRITAIN TIDY!

> I have a bit of a thing about rubbish. I hate the idea of people being lazy and just throwing their rubbish anywhere.
>
> I had an idea to design a litter bin that is a bit funny or quirky, in the hope that people might use it more and it would also draw attention to the message: please try to keep our city clean!
>
> So I designed the bunny bin. It's a bin that encourages passers-by to deposit their rubbish, rather than leaving it on the street. It is a five-foot-tall plastic rabbit that holds a beautifully illustrated bag in its paws. When the bag receives your rubbish the rabbit's ears light up, to thank you for your tidy behaviour.

I chose the rabbit because it's a symbol of good luck for me.
Years ago, I was travelling up to Nottingham with a friend
of mine, and I was daydreaming out the window.
When he asked, 'What are you looking for so intently?' I said,
'A rabbit – for good luck. If I see a rabbit my new collection
will sell really well.'

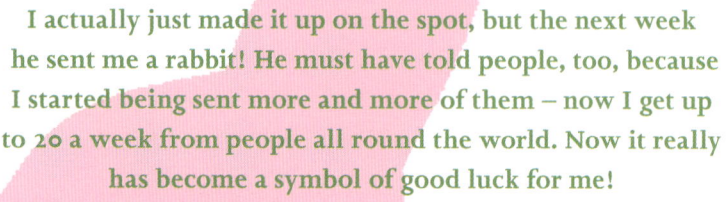

I actually just made it up on the spot, but the next week he sent me a rabbit! He must have told people, too, because I started being sent more and more of them – now I get up to 20 a week from people all round the world. Now it really has become a symbol of good luck for me!

The bin idea is hopefully a tiny hop towards making people think more about what they do with their rubbish. **,**

BIN THERE, DONE THAT...

Paul Smith is a sharp dresser, so it's perhaps no surprise that he'd like his surroundings equally well presented. Characteristic of his tailoring and design, **THE BUNNY BIN INCORPORATES PLAYFUL EMBELLISHMENTS AND DETAILING** that makes it stylish as well as functional.

Paul's bunny bin has been prototyped and was tested for several months in the busy shopping districts of London's Covent Garden and Holland Park. Made from moulded green plastic, the bunny stands at five feet high, holds patterned rubbish bags and has huge ears lit up by hundreds of tiny LED lights. Shop owners reported seeing noticeably less litter on the street whilst the bins were installed, leading to requests to have them placed there permanently. **THE TRIAL WENT SO WELL THAT THE BUNNY BIN MAY BE HOPPING ITS WAY ONTO A HIGH STREET NEAR YOU**. An example of the bin can be found in the foyer of London's Design Museum.

THINKING OUTSIDE THE 'BIN'

About 30 million tonnes of household waste are created in the UK every year. **THIS IS THE EQUIVALENT WEIGHT OF ALMOST 200,000 JUMBO JETS.** While Paul's bunny bin tries to encourage more use of London's bins, he could also reduce and re-use waste by using recycled products in his next collection.

For example, London-based shoe designers Above+Below use the leather, rubber and upholstery from old bus and train seats to make shoes. Paul could also make his bags from reclaimed material, following the example of Freitag, a Swiss company who negotiate with haulage companies to buy the tarpaulins which once covered the side of goods lorries. These are turned into bespoke bags, made to order for each customer. Customers can even choose which part of the tarpaulin their bag will be made from.

With ideas like these on the loose, who knows what will come next? Hats made from tyres? Jewellery from spare parts? Calling all fashionistas – take note! Goods lorries are next season's must-have accessory.

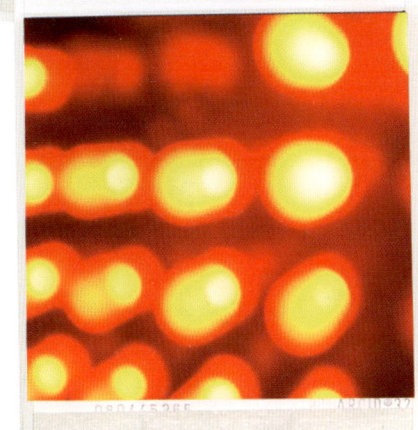

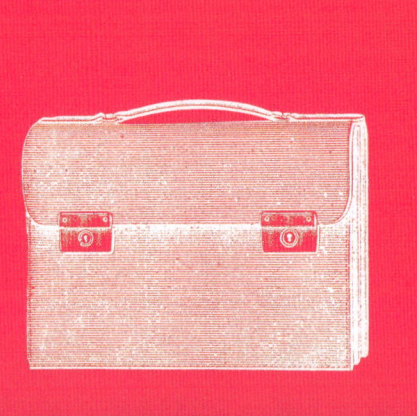

6. BUSINESS PEOPLE & PUBLIC FIGURES

PETER JONES
THE CAR-MOUNTED SHRINK RAY

ENTREPRENEUR AND MILLIONAIRE BUSINESSMAN PETER JONES BECAME A HOUSEHOLD NAME THROUGH HIS ROLE AS AN INVESTOR ON *DRAGONS' DEN*. NO STRANGER TO BACKING INNOVATIVE IDEAS, PETER IS ALSO A SELF-CONFESSED CAR NUT, AND HIS PASSION FOR DRIVING INSPIRED HIM TO INVENT THE CAR-MOUNTED SHRINK RAY.

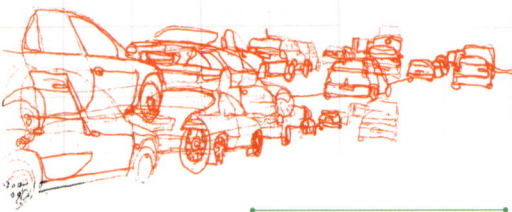

> I have always loved cars. I'm a big petrol head. The first car I owned was an orange Alfa Romeo Alfasud. It was my pride and joy, but it did highlight certain problems for me.
>
> Being 6 feet 7 inches tall I had some difficulty fitting into it, and, having squeezed into it, I then had problems getting out. I had to swing my legs out first, like a lady dismounting a horse, being careful not to damage the sills with my size-13 feet.
>
> Lots of cars aren't built for people as tall as I am. It's a nuisance. So I propose a Car-Mounted Shrink Ray. Then I could shrink myself down and easily fit into any car. I think I'd only need to be shrunk down to the size of, say, Richard Hammond or Theo Paphitis.

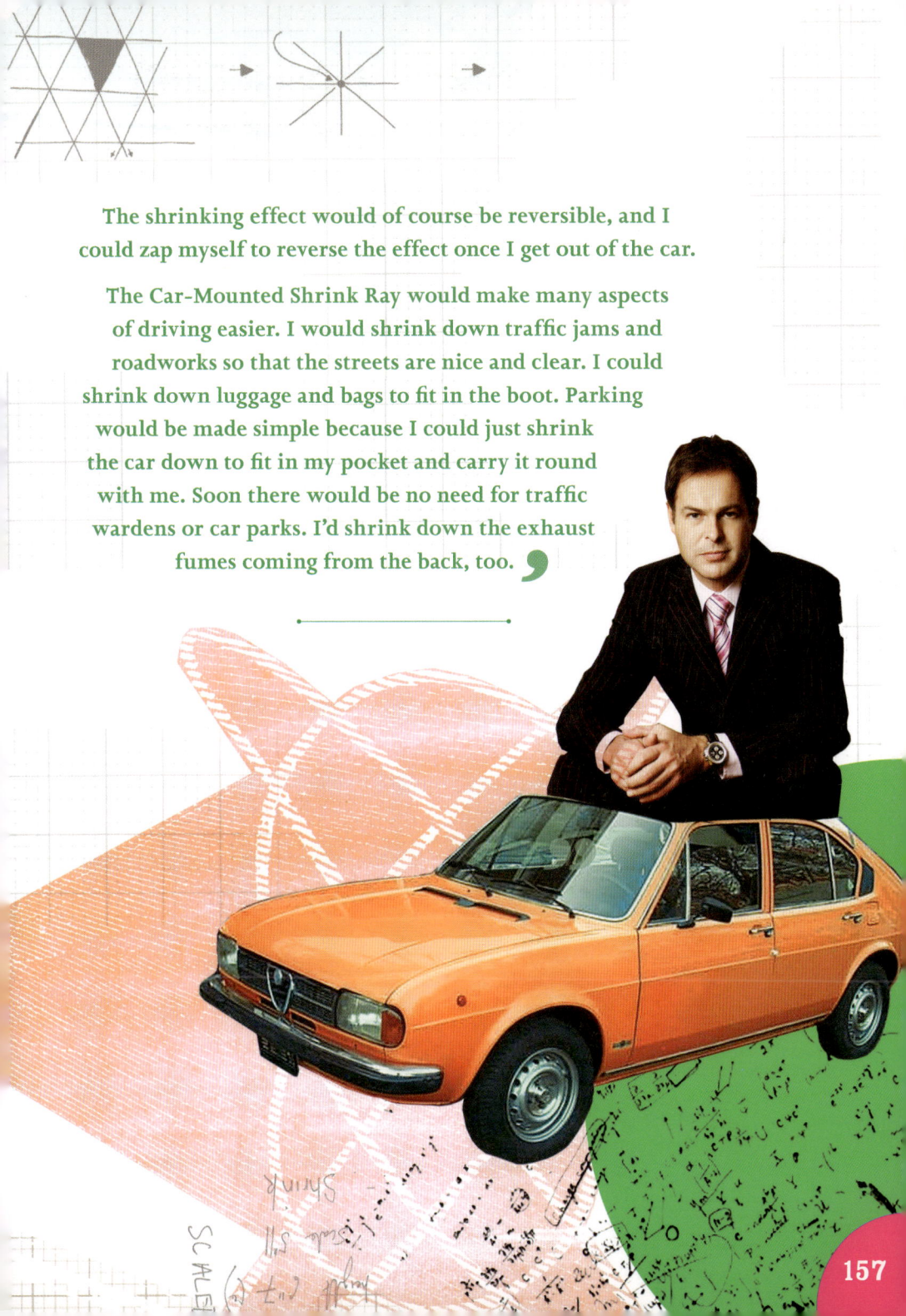

The shrinking effect would of course be reversible, and I could zap myself to reverse the effect once I get out of the car.

The Car-Mounted Shrink Ray would make many aspects of driving easier. I would shrink down traffic jams and roadworks so that the streets are nice and clear. I could shrink down luggage and bags to fit in the boot. Parking would be made simple because I could just shrink the car down to fit in my pocket and carry it round with me. Soon there would be no need for traffic wardens or car parks. I'd shrink down the exhaust fumes coming from the back, too.

HONEY, I SHRUNK PETER JONES!

Believe it or not, shrink rays might not be the stuff of Hollywood films and sci-fi fantasies. **SOME OF THE GREATEST SCIENTIFIC MINDS HAVE TURNED THEMSELVES TO THE TASK OF MINIATURIZING.**

However, biologist and philosopher Isaac Asimov argued that shrinking someone would have major effects on the body. Every part of every body is made up of atoms, which can't get any smaller. **SO IF A PERSON WERE SHRUNK, THEIR SMALLER ORGANS WOULD HAVE TO CONTAIN FEWER ATOMS.** That means that certain organs, like your brain and lungs, would be much less effective. If you were reduced to the size of an ant you would literally just stop working! **PETER WOULD HAVE TO BE EXTREMELY CAREFUL WITH THE SETTINGS ON HIS SHRINK RAY.**

Ok, so humans can't be shrunk, but there's no reason the Shrink Ray can't be used on some of life's other annoyances…

TO-SHRINK LIST

- ✓ The working week
- ✓ Bills
- ✓ Queue jumpers
- ✓ Dog poo
- ✓ Wasps
- ✓ Bankers' bonuses
- ✓ France

MARGARET THATCHER

SOFT-SCOOP ICE CREAM AND NEW INVENTION POLICY

MARGARET THATCHER SERVED AS PRIME MINSTER OF BRITAIN THROUGHOUT THE 1980s AND WAS RENOWNED FOR HER STEELY DETERMINATION AND UNCOMPROMISING ATTITUDE. FEW PEOPLE KNOW, HOWEVER, THAT THE IRON LADY HAD A 'SOFTER' SIDE…

Before entering into the world of politics, Margaret studied chemistry at Oxford University. Upon graduating she found work at food manufacturers J. Lyons and Co. as a research chemist. In the 1950s, as part of a small team, **SHE WAS TASKED WITH DEVELOPING A METHOD FOR WHIPPING MORE AIR INTO ICE CREAM.** The resulting invention produced what we now call **SOFT-SCOOP** ice cream.

Margaret's innovation slashed manufacturing costs by using fewer ingredients. Soft-scoop ice cream had the added benefit of increased consumer appeal, as **THE PUBLIC LOVED THE LIGHTER, SOFTER AND MORE MALLEABLE** texture of this new ice cream. It also had the advantage that it could be pumped and dispensed through a machine, giving ice cream a new lease of life and heralding the age of Mr Whippy ice-cream vans and the 99 Flake.

MONEY FOR NOTHING

J. Lyons and Co. were able to charge significantly more for Margaret's innovative new soft-scoop ice cream than for regular ice cream, **DESPITE THE FACT THAT IT WAS MADE FROM ABOUT 30% AIR.** Thanks to innovations such as soft scoop, in 2010 the global market for ice cream was a staggering £40 billion.

MARGARET'S INNOVATION FOR INVENTION

Through her experience at J. Lyons and Co., Margaret understood the power of a good idea. Consequently, when she came to be Prime Minister in the early 1980s she overturned a curious patenting policy that had originated as a result of the Second World War.

Remarkably, in order to secure 50 old American ships for the war effort, the UK Government had set up a policy that required anyone who had received public funding in researching their invention to sign their patent over to the Government.

The UK authorities then agreed with the US to abandon rights to three world-changing inventions, **FORFEITING HUNDREDS OF MILLIONS OF POUNDS** by agreeing not to patent radar, the jet engine and penicillin.

This policy was still in place in the early 1980s, forcing companies and universities who had received any state funding, however little, to hand over their idea for the Government to choose how to profit from it. Upon taking power, **MARGARET PROMPTLY ABOLISHED THIS POLICY**, opening the way for a flurry of innovation.

Under her period of office UK inventors created some of the world's most ubiquitous and influential inventions, and also one or two clangers:

1. The ARM group benefited greatly from Margaret's influence. The first ARM 32-bit microchip was made for the Acorn personal computer in 1985 and led to the development of a series of ever-more sophisticated microchips. As of 2005, about 98% of the more than one billion mobile phones sold each year use at least one ARM microchip.

2. Sir Clive Sinclair was a major beneficiary of Margaret's policies. In 1981 he launched Sinclair ZX81 Home Computer. With 1K of memory and 1K of RAM, 50,000 ZXs would be needed to run Microsoft Word or iTunes. However, this machine ushered in the start of the home-computing era, introducing a generation to the wonders of gaming and computer programming.

3. Riding high from his success, in 1985 Sir Clive produced the Sinclair C5, a battery-assisted tricycle, steered by a handlebar located beneath the driver's knees. Unfortunately, it was a spectacular flop. Perhaps one of the daftest inventions of the decade, it was intended for use on the road even though it sat only two feet high. It offered no protection from the weather, no crash protection and with a 15mph top speed proved too dangerous and impractical to catch on.

ADAM BALON

INNOCENT SMOOTHIES AND THE AMAZING ELECTRIC BATH

MOST PEOPLE ARE FAMILIAR WITH THE FACT THAT INNOCENT SMOOTHIES MAKE HEALTHY FRUIT DRINKS, BUT YOU MAY BE SURPRISED TO KNOW THAT THE TEAM BEHIND THIS HUGELY POPULAR DRINKS BRAND VERY NEARLY MADE A DIFFERENT PRODUCT ALTOGETHER.

Danger
High voltage

Adam Balon, one of Innocent's three founders, explains their idea:

'In 1999 my friends Jon, Richard and I decided that we'd like to go into business together. But at that stage, we didn't have a clear plan of what the business should do. So we thought about the problems that we faced every day, and tried to invent something to make life easier and better for everyone.

The first idea we came up with was for an electric bath. Essentially, it was a bath that would fill itself to your chosen level and temperature at the touch of a button. We got quite excited.

Because Richard's the marketing guy, he came up with the name: "The Amazing Electric Bath". I'm the sales guy, so I was already thinking about how we could sell it into hotel chains. Jon was especially excited because he's an engineer, so he started sketching out the technical drawings.

There was one problem with the electric bath, though. When we saw its preliminary sketches, we realized that it involved water and electricity in close proximity to each other. Rather than making life easier and better for people, we realized there was a risk we were going to make it shorter. That seemed to give it limited consumer appeal.

Shortly after the Electric Bath we settled on the idea of making smoothies.'

A SHOCKING IDEA?

As shrewd businessmen, Adam, Richard and Jon quickly arrested development on their Electric Bath idea, realizing its perceived shortcomings would make the bath very hard to sell.

However, the concept of a safe bath that regulates its temperature to make sure it's exactly as you would like it is a good one. In fact, as the Innocent founders initially thought, it would be reasonably straightforward (and not necessarily dangerous) to use an electronically controlled thermostat and a heating element to maintain the temperature of the bath.

The problem is that even if innocent could prove it was safe, **THEY'D STILL FIND AN ELECTRIC BATH A PRETTY HARD SELL.**

The Amazing Electric Bath started from a good concept, but because it would prove hard to commercialize, it was abandoned as a business proposition. However, **THE PATENT ARCHIVES ARE LITTERED WITH EXAMPLES OF DAFT INVENTIONS** that never made it to market and hopefully never will. Here are some of the weirdest:

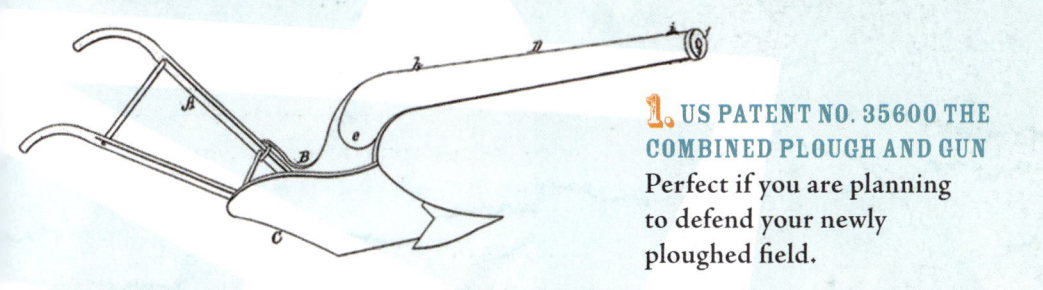

1. US PATENT NO. 35600 THE COMBINED PLOUGH AND GUN
Perfect if you are planning to defend your newly ploughed field.

2. US PATENT NO. 4278719 THE WATERPROOF TOWEL
Solves the problem of soggy towels, but creates the problem of not being able to dry things.

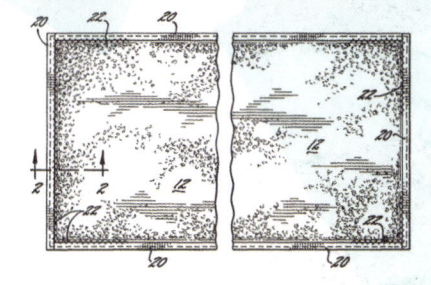

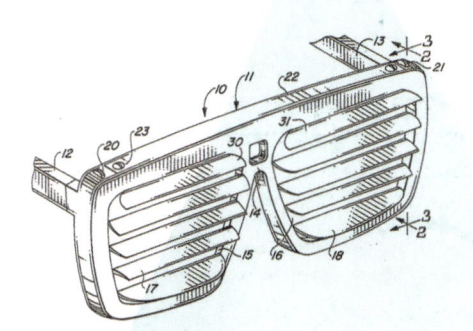

3. US PATENT NO. 4869584 VENETIAN BLIND SUNGLASSES
An ingenious way of making yourself look stupid.

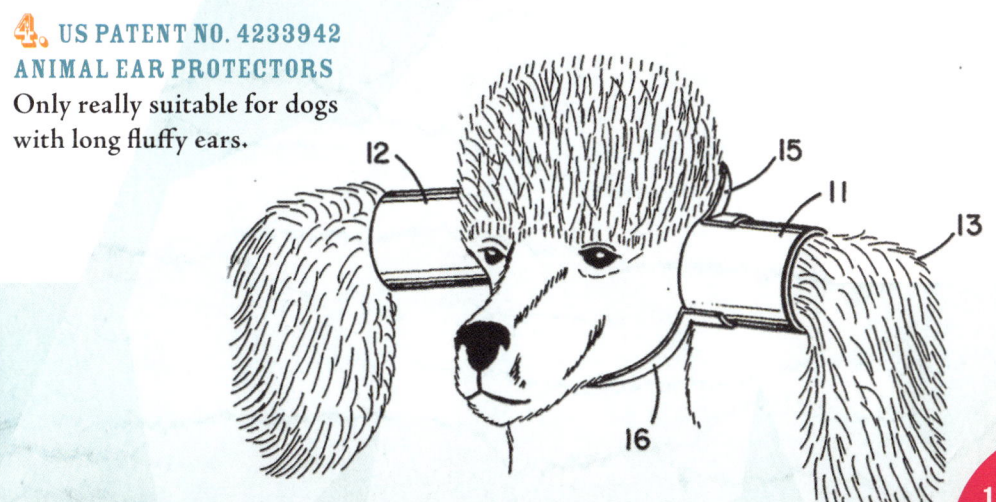

4. US PATENT NO. 4233942 ANIMAL EAR PROTECTORS
Only really suitable for dogs with long fluffy ears.

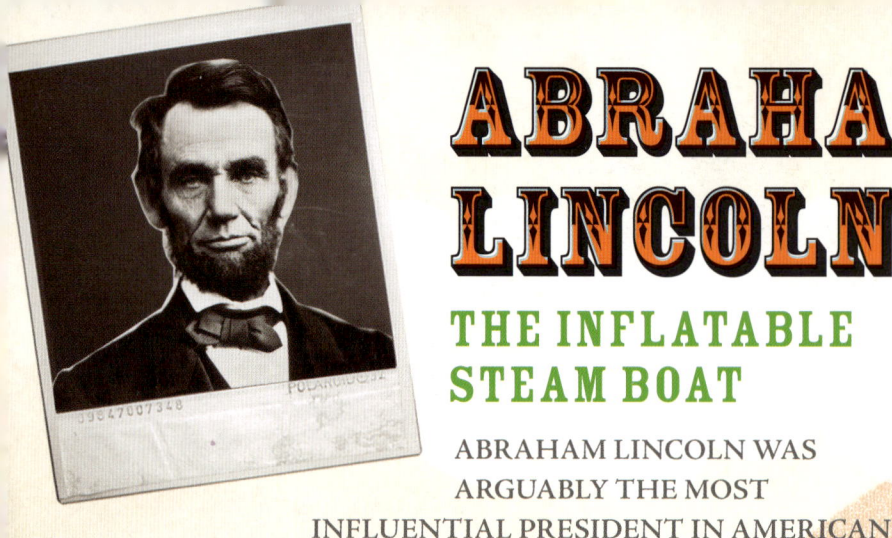

ABRAHAM LINCOLN

THE INFLATABLE STEAM BOAT

ABRAHAM LINCOLN WAS ARGUABLY THE MOST INFLUENTIAL PRESIDENT IN AMERICAN HISTORY, LEADING THE COUNTRY THROUGH THE CIVIL WAR AND ENDING SLAVERY. HOWEVER, HE WAS ALMOST KILLED BEFORE HE MADE IT INTO HIGH OFFICE, AND THIS NEAR-DEATH EXPERIENCE INSPIRED A REMARKABLE INVENTION THAT WOULD STILL SOUND WACKY IF IT WERE PROPOSED TODAY.

One stormy evening in 1849, Abraham was travelling by steamboat on the River Illinois when the boat snagged itself on a rock lying in the riverbed. **THE STEAMBOAT LURCHED OVER, ROLLING TO ONE SIDE AND ALMOST CATAPULTING ABRAHAM OVERBOARD.** Buffeted by the raging river, the boat was in real danger of sinking, taking the future president – now clinging on for dear life – with it.

Fast thinking was called for, and luckily the boat had a captain capable of just that. He issued a strange order, one that the vast majority of sailors won't hear in a lifetime – **HE ORDERED ALL THE EMPTY BARRELS STORED ONBOARD TO BE TIED TO THE BOAT'S SUNKEN SIDE,** just under the water. One by one these buoyed up the boat and eventually allowed it to float free.

The close call gave Abraham an idea for an invention. **HE PROPOSED THAT ALL STEAMBOATS SHOULD HAVE AN INFLATABLE SKIRT THAT COULD BE PUMPED FULL OF AIR,** which would raise the boat out of the water, and avoid any sandbanks or obstacles that might be lurking in its path. It's an idea that wouldn't look out of place in *Chitty Chitty Bang Bang*.

AHEAD OF HIS TIME

Fifty years before the invention of the hydrofoil and a century before the hovercraft, **ABRAHAM HAD RECOGNIZED THE ADVANTAGES OF REMOVING THE SHIP'S HULL FROM THE WATER AS FAR AS POSSIBLE.**

Although Abraham's invention was never commercialized, a model of his idea was created and is currently on display at the Smithsonian Museum of American History in Washington, DC.

Despite his invention not becoming a reality, **ABRAHAM NEVER LOST HIS ENTHUSIASM FOR NEW TECHNOLOGY,** and it was this passion that was instrumental in developing the US patent system.

In a speech to statesmen and inventors, Abraham called the development of patent laws **'ONE OF THE MOST IMPORTANT DEVELOPMENTS IN THE WORLD'S HISTORY'** and declared that it **'ADDED THE FUEL OF INTEREST TO THE FIRE OF GENIUS'.**

It's strange to think that such a sombre historical figure, no doubt with weighty political issues to consider, spent time inventing inflatable steamboats. Who knows what Barack Obama might be thinking?

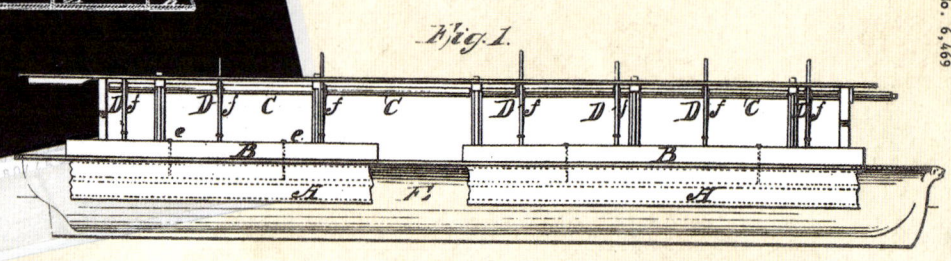

UNPRECEDENTED PRESIDENTIAL BRILLIANCE

Abraham Lincoln was not the only inventive politician to come from the United States. Founding father Benjamin Franklin invented **LIGHTNING RODS**, **BIFOCAL LENSES**, **FURNACE STOVES** and a strange musical instrument called a **GLASS ARMONICA**, which was a series of rotating, tuned glass cylinders played using a wet finger.

Third US president Thomas Jefferson, principal author of the Declaration of Independence, claimed to have invented the **LAZY SUSAN**, a revolving platter from which presidential dinner guests could choose their favourite dishes.

George W. Bush should probably be hailed as the greatest inventor of words since Shakespeare. During his time in office he gave life to words like **'EMBITTERMENT'**, **'BARIFF'**, **'COMPASSIONATED'** and **'MISUNDERESTIMATE'**, along with the classic sayings:

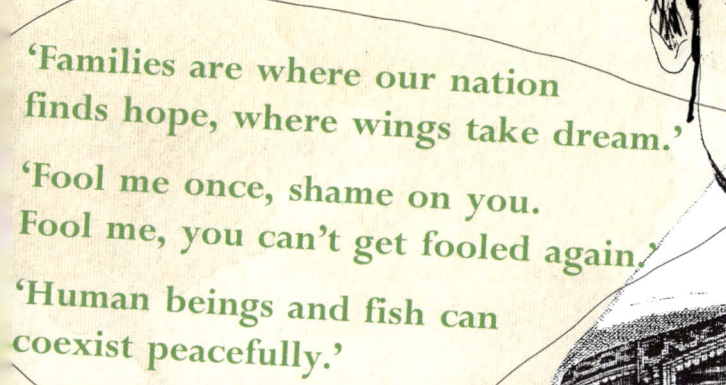

'Families are where our nation finds hope, where wings take dream.'

'Fool me once, shame on you. Fool me, you can't get fooled again.'

'Human beings and fish can coexist peacefully.'

MARTHA LANE FOX

THE LEVITATING WALKING STICK

BUSINESSWOMAN MARTHA LANE FOX CO-FOUNDED LASTMINUTE.COM, AN ICON OF THE DOTCOM BOOM OF THE EARLY 2000s. SHE IS NOW AN ADVISOR TO COMPANIES SUCH AS MARKS & SPENCER AND CHANNEL 4.

In May 2004 Martha was severely injured and spent a year in hospital. During her gradual recovery, Martha used a range of equipment and accessories to help her move again, and as a result has a smart invention idea – THE LEVITATING WALKING STICK.

One of the worst things about starting a travel company was that you were continuously tempted on amazing holidays but were always working so could never go on them. When I left lastminute.com I travelled a great deal and decided to drive to Morocco, as it is one of my favourite places.

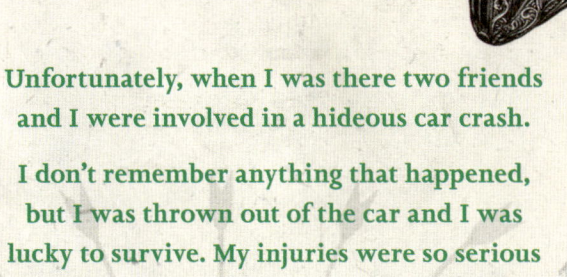

Unfortunately, when I was there two friends and I were involved in a hideous car crash.

I don't remember anything that happened, but I was thrown out of the car and I was lucky to survive. My injuries were so serious that I had to be flown back to the UK for emergency surgery, where I was literally put back together. My body is now full of metal — sometimes I feel like the bionic woman.

I have had to undergo lots of physiotherapy, and I now walk with a stick. In my daily life, I find that the most annoying sound in the world is that of my stick clunking on the floor! It's a real pain.

My idea for an invention is a levitating walking stick that can never fall over. It is designed to float about like something from Harry Potter, staying upright and by my side at all times. It works using electromagnets, to keep it upright, and a gyroscope, to keep it vertical. '

LEVITATION

Martha's idea is not just a dream from the pages of Harry Potter; remarkably, a number of different techniques have been developed and are SUCCESSFULLY USED TO MAKE OBJECTS LEVITATE.

Perhaps the most commonly used is, as Martha suggested, 'MAGNETIC LEVITATION', or 'MAGLEV'. This uses a magnetic force to counteract gravity and cause objects to seemingly float.

Maglev trains have been developed and THE FIRST COMMERCIAL HIGH-SPEED MAGLEV LINE IN THE WORLD HAS BEEN INSTALLED from Shanghai Pudong International Airport in China. Since the train floats above the rails, it is faster (over 500km/h), quieter and smoother than wheeled versions.

There are a couple of drawbacks to using Maglev technology to make things levitate. First, it is horrendously expensive: the

Pudong line in China cost **£45 MILLION PER MILE**. The second drawback is that the levitating object can only move where Maglev lines have been built, which doesn't make it ideal for use with a walking stick. Unless you have a very particular route in mind…

NOT SO FAR-FETCHED?

Despite the Maglev not being a viable way of developing Martha's idea, **THE CONCEPT OF A LEVITATING STICK MAY NOT ACTUALLY BE SO FAR-FETCHED.** Researchers at Japan's Kobe Gakuin University have invented a levitating wheelchair that hovers on a small cushion of air, and they believe **THE TECHNIQUE COULD BE USED TO MAKE ALL KINDS OF OBJECTS FLOAT,** including walking sticks.

The prototype wheelchair, inspired by arcade air-hockey games, shoots jets of air out of many openings beneath a sports-style car seat on a platform. This means the seat can be pushed around easily. The jets are carefully controlled to prevent excessive vertical movement of the chair, so there is no danger of the seat taking off or troubling air-traffic control.

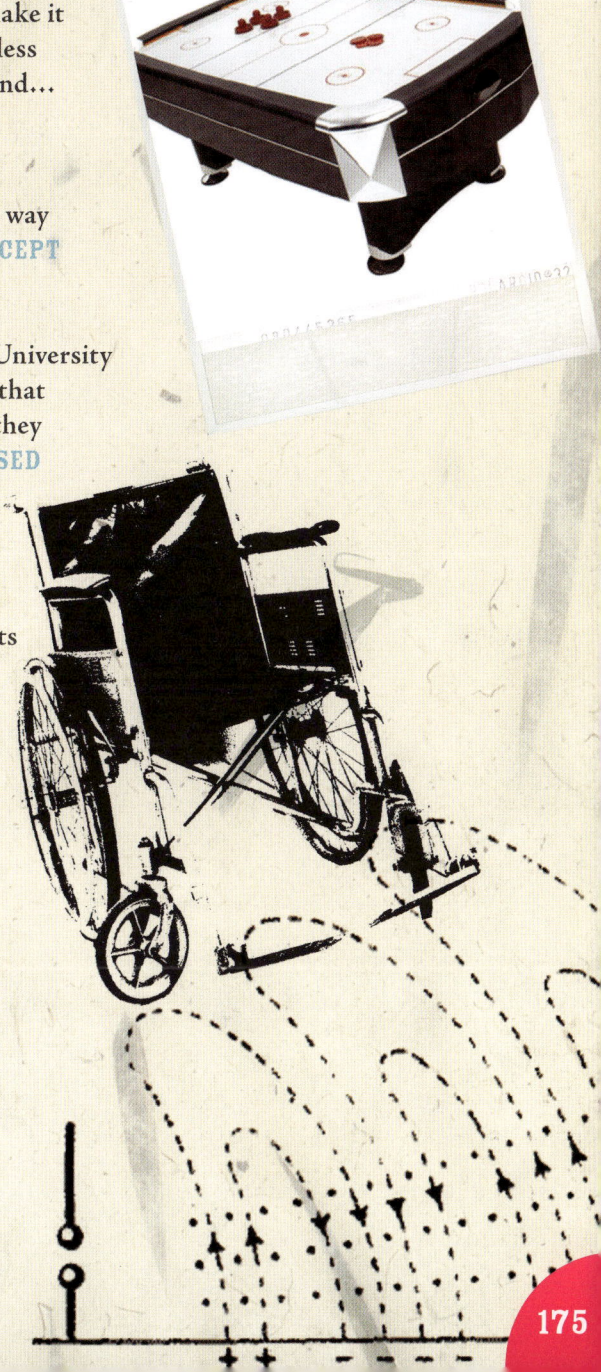

175

SIMON WOODROFFE

ROBOTIC SHOE SHOPS

ENTREPRENEUR SIMON WOODROFFE STARTED OUT AS A ROADIE FOR THE LIKES OF ROD STEWART AND THE MOODY BLUES BEFORE FOUNDING RESTAURANT CHAIN YO! SUSHI.

His Japanese restaurants make use of innovations such as **ROBOT DRINKS TROLLEYS, SELF-SERVE BEER TAPS** and **SELF-HEATING PLATES.** These innovations have given Simon the idea for an invention to improve the humble shoe shop, with a similar injection of new technology.

' I really like shoes, particularly brightly coloured ones. I bought a lime-green pair about ten years ago and never looked back! I love how shoe design is always moving forward: trainer design constantly makes use of new materials and increasingly sophisticated manufacturing techniques, making shoes better and better.

However, the experience of buying shoes in a shop hasn't really changed at all. Think about how you currently buy them. You walk into a store and are met with these rather naffly displayed shoes. All the different sizes are kept in boxes out of sight and store workers have to go and fetch them repeatedly. There must be a better way of doing it.

My invention is a whole new type of shoe shop. All the shoeboxes are stacked from floor to ceiling, and a robotic arm moves up and down, and pulls the right box out. You can see the robots in action, whizzing to and fro, gathering shoes. You can control them yourself, at the touch of a button. It'd be great fun.

> I believe you could take any business in the world and come up with a way of completely changing it around, and my invention revolutionizes shoe shopping!

As a motivational speaker and wealthy entrepreneur, Simon believes that to be successful in business you need to be **'OUTRAGEOUS'**. This is clearly demonstrated in his proposed robotic shoe shops idea (and his footwear). Having founded Japanese-style micro-hotels (Yotels), started a radio station and brought conveyor belts into his sushi restaurants, it's clear he lives by this philosophy.

HOW MIGHT THE ROBOTIC SHOE SHOP WORK?

There are a number of different industrial robots that Simon could use to fit out his robotic shoe shops, but perhaps the most suitable would be the SCARA.

SCARA robots are mechanical arms capable of swift and precise movement. They are often used to pick and pack products in a factory, and would be ideal for retrieving shoeboxes in Simon's shops.

UNIQUELY USELESS

Simon's invention and his famous sushi enterprise are heavily influenced by advancements made in Japan. **THIS COUNTRY IS WELL KNOWN FOR ITS TECHNOLOGICAL INVENTIVENESS,** and has brought us some of the best innovations in recent years, but Simon has avoided a whole category of Japanese invention that is slightly less useful to the world…

This is known as **CHINDOGU** – which literally translates as 'useless invention'.

CHINDOGU HALL OF FAME

Believe it or not, these inventions are all commercially available:

1. THE ALL-DAY TISSUE DISPENSER: A toilet roll fixed on top of a hat, for hay-fever sufferers.

2. SHOE UMBRELLAS: Individual mini-umbrellas fitted to the end of your shoes to stop them getting wet.

3. DUSTER SLIPPERS FOR CATS: So they can help out with the housework.

4. FUNNEL SPECS: Glasses with funnels fitted instead of lenses to allow eye drops to be administered with ease.

5. THE ALL-OVER PLASTIC BATHING COSTUME: To enable people who suffer from aquaphobia to swim without coming into contact with water.

PRINCE CHARLES

WINE-FUELLED ASTON MARTIN

HEIR TO THE THRONE PRINCE CHARLES IS A CHAMPION FOR SUSTAINABLE LIVING. HE HAS STATED THAT HE IS DETERMINED TO DO AS MUCH AS HE CAN TO CUT HIS CARBON FOOTPRINT, SAVE ENERGY AND PROTECT THE ENVIRONMENT. THIS HAS RESULTED IN A BIZARRE INVENTION – A WINE-FUELLED ASTON MARTIN.

In order to reduce his motoring emissions, Prince Charles's Aston Martin Volante, a twenty-first-birthday present from the Queen, has been **CONVERTED TO RUN ON FUEL MADE ENTIRELY FROM ENGLISH WINE.** This is an environmentally friendly act in more ways than one, as the EU sets strict limits on wine production and any excess is not allowed to be sold on the market. But to prevent wasting it, one way in which it can be redistributed is for use as bioethanol environmental fuel.

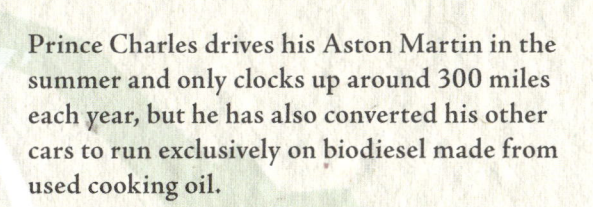

Prince Charles drives his Aston Martin in the summer and only clocks up around 300 miles each year, but he has also converted his other cars to run exclusively on biodiesel made from used cooking oil.

Environmental fuels such as biodiesel and bioethanol are popular alternatives to diesel and petrol, and in fact bioethanol commonly replaces petrol. **BIOETHANOL CAN BE MADE FROM FERMENTED FRUIT OR PLANT PARTS** (ethanol being the alcohol in the wine), and most petrol-driven cars can run on 10% bioethanol without any alteration. However, they can all be converted to run entirely on this fuel just like Prince Charles's Aston Martin.

VINTAGE CHIC

It's not just Charles's Aston that is a classic updated for the modern age: as part of his green lifestyle **CHARLES SAYS HE HAS TAKEN TO WEARING SECOND-HAND 'VINTAGE' CLOTHES** and ensuring that as many of his garments as possible last a lifetime.

181

He has professed to enjoy 'upcycling' – taking old clothes and refashioning them with a modern twist – and he regularly wears a pair of shoes made from leather salvaged from an eighteenth-century shipwreck off the British coast, which he reckons is 'totally indestructible'.

CLEAN AND GREEN

Alongside his wine-powered Aston and vintage fashion, Prince Charles has adopted a whole range of innovative measures to ensure his royal residences are as green as possible.

At Highgrove, **THE PRINCE USES COLLECTED RAINWATER TO FLUSH THE ROYAL TOILETS** and instead of fibreglass insulation, he uses lambs' wool. His windows are double-glazed and he has installed solar panels to further reduce his carbon emissions.

In fact, Prince Charles is so concerned about this issue that he even **FEEDS HIS COWS ON GRASS RATHER THAN GRAIN,** to reduce their methane 'emissions'.

182

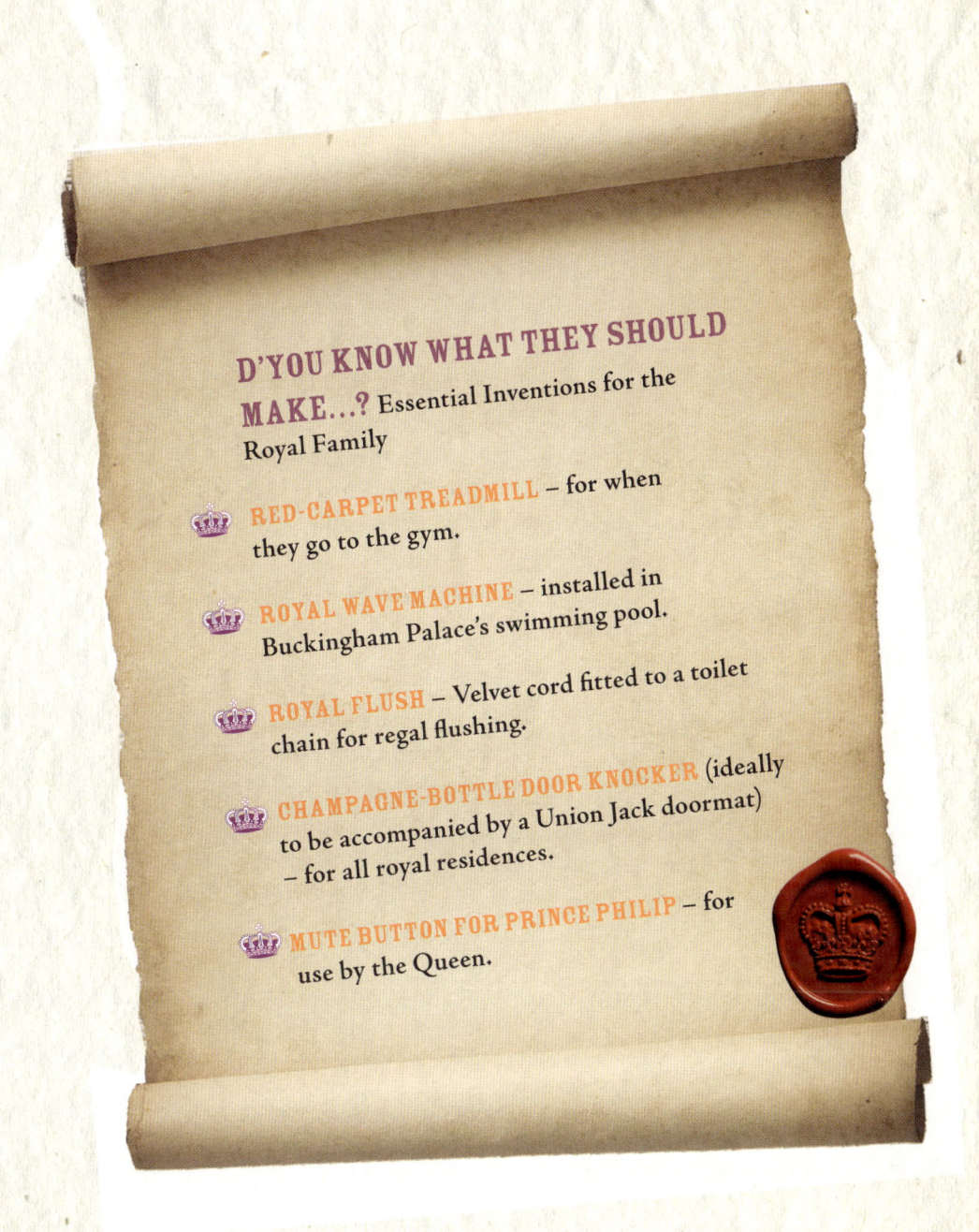

D'YOU KNOW WHAT THEY SHOULD MAKE...? Essential Inventions for the Royal Family

- **RED-CARPET TREADMILL** – for when they go to the gym.

- **ROYAL WAVE MACHINE** – installed in Buckingham Palace's swimming pool.

- **ROYAL FLUSH** – Velvet cord fitted to a toilet chain for regal flushing.

- **CHAMPAGNE-BOTTLE DOOR KNOCKER** (ideally to be accompanied by a Union Jack doormat) – for all royal residences.

- **MUTE BUTTON FOR PRINCE PHILIP** – for use by the Queen.

TONY BENN
THE SEATCASE AND OTHERS

FORMER CABINET MINISTER TONY BENN HAS SPENT NEARLY HALF A CENTURY AS AN MP. AS MINISTER FOR TECHNOLOGY, IN THE 1960s HE WAS INVOLVED IN A WIDE RANGE OF WELL-KNOWN HI-TECH PROJECTS, INCLUDING THE DEVELOPMENT OF CONCORDE AND INTERNATIONAL COMPUTERS LTD. WHAT IS LESS WELL KNOWN IS THAT HE IS ALSO AN AVID INVENTOR.

'I like to look at things to see if they can be improved. Often when I face a problem, I'll look to see if anything can solve it, and if that's impossible, I'll adapt it to suit my needs. In 1981 I was struck down with Guillain-Barre syndrome, which reduced my ability to stand for long periods, so I invented the Seatcase.

I had to carry a stool and a rucksack around with me at all times and one day it occurred to me that life would be much easier if I combined the two. They are very useful if I'm waiting for a bus, or if there's no free seat on the Tube, as I'm still able to sit comfortably. It's heavenly.

Like most sensible ideas, the design is very simple and completely functional. In its developmental stages I created a whole army of prototypes (most of which are now cluttering up my house!) to boil it down to the essential components.

I think if the Seatcase were made well it would be very popular. I'm looking for a business partner to commercialize it at the moment.

In fact, I sent the Seatcase to Richard Branson recently. I suggested he could use the slogan "Virgin gives you a seat from your home to your destination". I haven't heard back yet.

Tony's character and role as Minister for Technology suggest that **HE IS A PROBLEM SOLVER WITH A LOVE OF INNOVATION**, which is backed up by the fact that he has been inventing products for his home and office throughout his life. Here are some intriguing, if not altogether safe, examples of other ideas he has had:

1. CAR-MOUNTED CHAIR:

When starting out in politics, Tony took to canvassing the streets in a chair tied to the top of his car. This 'drive-by electioneering' involved Tony perched on top of his car proclaiming his message to unsuspecting passers-by with the help of a megaphone. This seemed to work well enough, as he won the Bristol South East seat in the 1950 by-election.

2. BRIEFCASE LECTERN:

In 1967, when Tony was a minister in Harold Wilson's government, he converted his ministerial briefcase so that it could be used as a lectern for public speaking (should he be called upon to give an impromptu speech). The converted briefcase provides the perfect surface for holding lecture notes simply by opening the case and removing a board that slots inside two grooves and props up the lid.

3. STATIONERY HOLDER:

Tony created a custom pencil case to keep his stationery perfectly arranged in his jacket pocket, so he could access the right pen without looking.

4. MAGNETIC CAR MAP:

Parking near his house in West London was so difficult that Tony made a magnetized map of the surrounding streets and placed it in his hallway. He and his wife had metal tokens to represent their cars and when they returned home, they would stick the tokens on the appropriate street so they could let each other know where they had parked their cars.

WRITTEN BY...
MARK CHAMPKINS

Mark Champkins is a designer and inventor based in London. He is a former **BRITISH INVENTOR OF THE YEAR** and is the founder of **CONCENTRATE,** a business that identifies inventive ways in which people can be inspired to be at their best and most focused.

In 2007 Mark successfully pitched Concentrate on the **BBC'S DRAGONS' DEN** and won investment from Peter Jones for his plans to launch a range of products that help children to focus in the classroom and get the most from their education.

Now a reality, these include:
THE BOTTLECOOLERPENHOLDER: a thermally insulating, wetsuit-style jacket for water bottles which also stores stationery so it acts as a reminder to drink plenty of water whilst working, as 2% dehydration leads to a 20% drop in concentration.

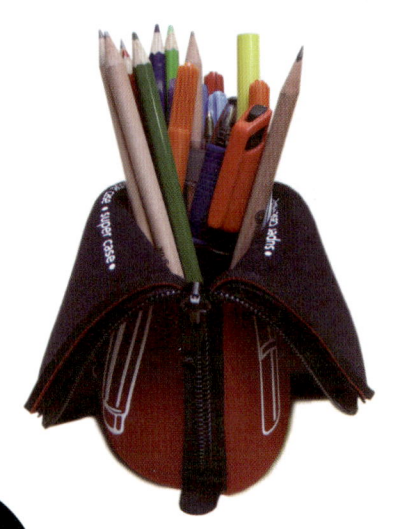

THE CHAIRPADBAG: a bag that doubles as a padded seat cover, to make hard plastic chairs more comfortable.

THE FOOD FOR THOUGHT LUNCHBOX: encourages pupils to eat a piece of fruit by protecting apples and bananas from being bruised.

THE VOTING RULER: encourages greater participation in lessons. It's a ruler with a green 'yes' at one end and a red 'no' on the other. Pupils can vote by holding the appropriate end in the air.

ANTI-SMELL SPORTS BAGS: a drawstring sports bag complete with activated carbon 'pong patch' to absorb smell and moisture. Makes wearing PE kits that have been stored in a locker more appealing to all.

PRE-CHEWED PENCILS: to remind kids when they are drifting off and about to chomp on their pencil.

189

His other inventions and design collaborations include:

SELF-HEATING CROCKERY: self-heating plates and bowls that heat up to sixty degrees at the touch of a button. The crockery will keep warm for 30 minutes, and can be recharged and reused over and over by simply being washed in hot water or cleaned in a dishwasher (2002/03 British Invention of the Year).

DESIGNING KITCHENWARE FOR JAMIE OLIVER to encourage young people to learn to cook. These include chopping-board recipe mats, various cooking utensils, Russian doll-style containers, magnetic chopping boards and gun-slinger aprons.

ADSPECS: $5 glasses with liquid-filled lenses whose prescription can be changed – these are designed for use in developing countries to correct children's eyesight and enable them to engage with the education system.

pre-chewed pencil

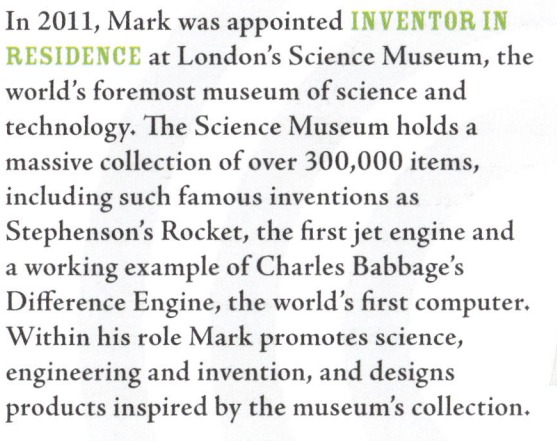

In 2011, Mark was appointed **INVENTOR IN RESIDENCE** at London's Science Museum, the world's foremost museum of science and technology. The Science Museum holds a massive collection of over 300,000 items, including such famous inventions as Stephenson's Rocket, the first jet engine and a working example of Charles Babbage's Difference Engine, the world's first computer. Within his role Mark promotes science, engineering and invention, and designs products inspired by the museum's collection.

He also founded an innovative website called the **MINISTRY OF INVENTION** www.ministryofinvention.co.uk to fund and provide support for students, teachers and would-be inventors with innovative ideas.

Contact mark@concentrate.org.uk for more information on the ideas and inventions.

THANK YOU

- Jerram Clifford
- Martin Vowles
- Anna Valentine
- Becky Glass
- Chris Terry
- Jemma Green
- Gideon Todes
- Clare Aitken
- Charley Boorman
- All those in the Studio, namely Alex Hammond, Gavin O'Carroll, Jitesh Patel, Vishal Shah, Nina Gritzke and Marie Cohen-Skalli
- Tony Benn and Ruth Winstone
- Nicola Roberts and Angela O'Connor
- Amy Green and all at The Kumara Corporation
- And finally all the celebrities and their teams who graciously agreed to contribute their invention ideas.

This book was illustrated by Jerram Clifford.

Jerram is an illustrator and image-maker who lives and works in North London. Originally from North Yorkshire, Jerram has studied internationally and specializes in mixed-media collage and photomontage. Throughout this book, Jerram has created surreal collages using a combination of hand-rendered and digital techniques. If you'd like to see more, visit:

www.jerram-clifford.com   jerramclifford@yahoo.co.uk